THE 30-DAY WHOLE FOOD COOKBOOK FOR BEGINNERS

Unleash the Power of Nature in Your Kitchen with Wholesome Meals That Are Perfect for Busy Lifestyles and Hungry Families

Azalea Landry

TABLE OF CONTENTS

CHAPTER 1: INTRODUCTION TO WHOLE FOOD EATING

1.1 THE FUNDAMENTALS OF WHOLE FOOD NUTRITION

Picture this: You walk through the aisles of your local grocery store and are greeted by a rainbow of fresh produce, bulk bins laden with grains and legumes, and the rich aroma of fresh herbs and spices. This, in essence, is whole food nutrition—a world where every natural color and texture promises not just an adventure for your taste buds but a bounty of benefits for your body.

In this chapter, we'll unpack the fundamentals of whole food nutrition, a cornerstone of health that embraces foods in their purest forms—untainted by artificial additives, preservatives, or processing that can strip away their natural goodness. Understanding these fundamentals isn't merely a quest for knowledge; it's the foundation for transforming your health, bite by wholesome bite.

The Essence of Whole Foods

Whole foods refer to foods that have been processed or refined as minimally as possible. They are free from additives or other artificial substances; think fruits, vegetables, grains, legumes, nuts, and seeds. They also include responsibly-sourced meat, fish, and dairy that haven't been laden with hormones or antibiotics. Essentially, if nature made it and humans haven't significantly tampered with it, it's a whole food.

Nutritional Superiority

Imagine that each whole food you consume is a symphony of nutrients playing in perfect harmony. The nutrients found in whole foods are complex and complete—unlike their refined counterparts or supplements. Vitamins, minerals, phytonutrients, fiber, and more, all exist within whole foods in ratios that nature intended. This natural balance ensures optimal absorption and use by the body, supporting everything from immune function to mental clarity.

The Fiber Factor

Let's talk about fiber, a prolific yet often overlooked nutrient found generously in whole foods. Beyond its well-known role in digestive health, fiber acts as a broom, sweeping through our insides to aid in the elimination of toxins and waste. It's also a champion for heart health and blood sugar regulation, and it keeps us feeling sated, which can prevent overeating. Whole grains, vegetables, and legumes stand as fiber's poster children, ready to contribute to a potent, healthful diet.

Phytonutrients - Nature's Gift

Whole foods naturally house an array of compounds known as phytonutrients or phytochemicals. These substances, which include antioxidants, flavonoids, and carotenoids, are the body's allies in warding off illness. They combat inflammation, act as antioxidants, and have various roles in preventing chronic diseases. The deep purples of berries, the vibrant oranges of carrots, and the lush greens of kale are all indicators of phytonutrient presence, each bringing its unique health-protecting properties.

A Minimalist Approach to Processing

While processing in itself isn't inherently bad—after all, cooking is a form of processing—over-processing is where we encounter problems. This includes stripping grains of their nutrient-rich layers to create white flour or adding sweeteners and preservatives to foods to enhance taste and shelf life at the expense of nutrition. Whole food nutrition encourages minimal processing to preserve natural goodness.

Balancing Macronutrients

In a whole food diet, macronutrients—proteins, carbohydrates, and fats—are ingested in their most healthful forms. Proteins come from lean meats, beans, and nuts; carbohydrates from complex, fiber-rich grains and vegetables; and fats from sources like avocados, nuts, and seeds, which offer healthy unsaturated versions. Balancing these macronutrients is key to sustained energy, cellular repair, and overall health.

Essential Diversity

One of the joys of whole foods is the variety they offer. Unlike restrictive diets that cut out entire food groups, whole food nutrition encourages diversity. This assortment ensures a broad spectrum of nutrients, reduces the risk of food intolerances, and keeps meals exciting and flavorful. It may mean venturing out of your culinary comfort zone, but the rewards to your palate and your health are vast.

The Anti-Inflammatory Influence

Many chronic diseases can be traced back to inflammation. The standard American diet, heavy in processed foods, can exacerbate this issue. Whole foods, on the other hand, are often inherently anti-inflammatory. This is especially true for plant-based whole foods, which not only prevent inflammation but can also reverse it, contributing to the prevention and management of chronic illnesses.

Sustainability—Beyond Nutrition

Whole food nutrition is not only about promoting health but also about honoring our planet. Sustainable eating means choosing foods that have less environmental impact—foods grown without harmful pesticides and practices that degrade soil and water. It's a responsible choice for your body and the earth, ensuring that the sources of our nourishment are preserved for future generations.

Harmony with the Seasons

Harvesting foods in their natural seasonality aligns whole food consumption with the rhythms of nature. It's not only poetic but practical—seasonal foods are often fresher, packed with more nutrients, and are an expression of the local agricultural landscape. Learning to relish foods that are in season is part of a holistic approach to nutrition, one that embraces timely variety and the cyclical beauty of nature.

The Challenge of Modern Living

It's important to acknowledge the tension between our busy modern lives and the practice of whole food nutrition. While it's true that convenience foods save time, they often do so at the cost of nutrition. Whole food nutrition requires a mindset shift, one that views food preparation not as a chore but as an act of self-care. It calls for a reallocation of priorities, placing the quality of the fuel we feed ourselves and our families at the top.

Marrying Convenience and Wholeness

Despite the challenges, there are strategies to harmonize whole food nutrition with a modern lifestyle. Meal planning, batch cooking, and the embrace of simple, yet nutrient-dense meals can streamline the process. Leveraging the power of a colorful salad, a robust soup, or a versatile grain bowl allows for nourishment without complexity. It's about finding that sweet spot where health and convenience coexist.

In conclusion, the fundamentals of whole food nutrition form a mosaic of benefits that stand the test of time. It's a return to basics, to the kind of eating that our bodies intuitively recognize and thrive on. Whether you're motivated by health concerns or just a desire for food that truly satisfies, embracing whole foods is a step toward vitality that cannot be replicated by a dietary supplement or a quick-fix diet. It's a loving nod to tradition mixed with the wisdom of modern science—a recipe for a life well-lived, one whole meal at a time.

1.2 THE BENEFITS OF A WHOLE FOOD DIET ON HEALTH AND WELL-BEING

When we embark on the vibrant journey of whole food eating, we're really setting the table for a lifelong feast of benefits that nourish not just our bodies, but our overall well-being. Whole foods are nature's treasures: unrefined and unprocessed ingredients that are as close to their natural state as possible. By incorporating these gems into our daily meals, we stand to reap a cornucopia of health rewards that are as diverse as the colors on our plates.

A Symphony of Nutrients

Whole foods are the virtuosos of nutrition, bringing a complex array of vitamins, minerals, fiber, and antioxidants to the orchestra of our bodily functions. Unlike their processed counterparts, they deliver these nutrients in their natural forms, often accompanied by a host of phytochemicals—those little-known plant compounds playing a supportive melody for our health. These nutritional powerhouses work in concert to bolster our immune system, fighting off the dissonant notes of illness and chronic diseases.

Digestive Harmony and Gut Health

Imagine your gut as a finely-tuned instrument, one that requires the right kind of fuel to play smoothly. Whole foods are that perfect pitch. High in fiber, they conduct the rhythms of our digestive system with care, preventing the jarring interruptions of constipation and irregularity. They help compose a healthy microbiome—the community of beneficial bacteria in our gut—thus orchestrating a balance that researchers increasingly link to numerous aspects of our well-being, from mood regulation to immune function.

The Resonance of Weight Management

In a world where fad diets crescendo and fall with the regularity of a metronome, whole food eating offers a stable, harmonious rhythm. It's not a diet but a way of life that naturally leads to a healthy weight. Whole foods, rich in fiber and nutrients, tend to be more satisfying and less calorie-dense. This means you can fill your plate with a bountiful arrangement of foods that satiate your hunger and help keep those unwanted pounds at bay without the need for calorie-counting.

The Sweet Sound of Stable Blood Sugar

Maintaining steady blood sugar levels is akin to keeping a steady beat in music—necessary for the performance to go on without a hitch. Whole foods, particularly those low in the glycemic index, release energy slowly and steadily. They prevent the sharp spikes and crashes associated with refined sugars, supporting not only a stable mood but also long-term health, reducing the risk of type 2 diabetes and heart disease.

A Crescendo in Heart Health

The heart keeps time for our body, and whole foods offer the nutrients necessary for keeping its rhythm robust. Whole grains, nuts, and seeds, as well as fruits and vegetables, are replete with heart-loving elements like soluble fiber, which helps reduce cholesterol, and potassium, which aids in blood pressure regulation. Indeed, embracing whole foods may be one of the most poignant ballads we sing for our heart's health.

The Clear Tone of Improved Mental Clarity

Nutrition and brain health are tightly interlaced, with whole foods playing a critical leading role in maintaining and enhancing cognitive function. The fatty acids found in fish, nuts, and seeds, for instance, act as building blocks for brain cells, while antioxidants in fruits and vegetables protect against oxidative stress, which can cloud our mental faculties. Through a diet rich in whole foods, we can clear the fog and stay sharp and focused.

The Melody of Skin and Beauty

Our skin, the body's largest organ, is often a reflection of what's happening on the inside. Whole foods are brimming with vitamins, such as A, C, and E, which are essential for skin health. They help protect against premature aging and promote a natural glow. So yes, that radiance you've noticed isn't a trick of the light—it's the result of a harmonious relationship with whole food nutrition.

Sustainable Energy for Life's Rhythms

Life is an endless cycle of crescendos and decrescendos, with our energy levels often struggling to keep up. Whole foods provide a sustainable energy source, rich in complex carbohydrates and proteins that help us maintain our tempo throughout the day. So, rather than reaching for a short-lived caffeine surge, whole food eating enables a natural vitality that sustains us from dawn until dusk.

Detoxifying Dynamics

Our bodies are equipped with a natural detoxification system that works tirelessly to maintain harmony. Whole foods support this intrinsic mechanism, delivering a rich variety of nutrients that help our liver, kidneys, and other organs to filter out the dissonant toxins, keeping us in tune and in health.

Strengthening Life's Ensemble

Bone health might not top the chart of our immediate concerns, but it plays a foundational role in the symphony of our health. From the calcium and magnesium in leafy greens to the vitamin D found in fortified whole food options, these dietary players come together to fortify the skeletal structure that supports us, ensuring we can dance through life with strength and vitality.

The Harmony of Longevity

While we might not yet have the sheet music to eternal life, a whole food diet is rich in the notes known to extend our lifespan. These foods, abundant in antioxidants and anti-inflammatory properties, are linked to a reduced risk of many chronic diseases—like strokes, heart disease, and certain cancers. In this way, choosing whole foods may help us not only add years to our life but, more critically, life to our years.

Embracing whole food nutrition is akin to finding our rhythm in the vast symphony of life's choices. It's the deep breath before a powerful chorus—transformative, life-enhancing, and radiating with promise. It's not about rigidity or unrealistic standards, but discovering a sustainable cadence that parallels the natural ebbs and flows of our existence.

Here's to the harmonious journey we're on toward whole health and vibrant well-being, one nourishing bite at a time. Whole food eating isn't merely a passage in the greater composition of life; it is an elemental tune that, once mastered, reverberates with endless layers of benefits, from the delicate whisper of prevention to the robust chorus of vitality and joy.

1.3 How to Transition to Whole Food Eating

Embarking on the journey of whole food eating can be a transformative, profoundly nourishing experience both for you and your family. It's about connecting with the vibrant spectrum of flavors offered by nature's pantry and letting those colors and textures infuse vitality into your meals—and, by extension, your life. But as with any meaningful change, the transition to a whole food diet carries its own set of challenges and considerations. Sit back and envision this as more than a dietary shift; it's about crafting a sustainable lifestyle that breathes wellness and energy into every facet of your day.

The allure of processed foods, replete with their ease and quick prep time, is strong in today's fast-paced world. Yet, they often come at a hidden cost to our health and well-being. Whole foods, in contrast, are those that have been minimally processed or refined, and they do not have additives such as sugars, salts, or fats. They include fruits, vegetables, whole grains, nuts, seeds, and lean meats, which are bursting with the nutrients needed to power your body and mind.

Easing into whole food eating doesn't have to be an insurmountable hurdle. In fact, it can be a joyful exploration of tastes and a rekindling of a connection with the food you consume. Here are some strategies to help you transition smoothly and sustainably:

Understand Your 'Why'

Identify your reasons for making this change. Do you desire more energy, a stronger immune system, or perhaps a way to naturally manage weight? Maybe it's a combination of factors or a hope to inspire your family to join you in healthier habits. Anchor yourself to your vision of better health like a tree roots into nourishing earth—it will be your stability when the winds of old habits and convenience foods gust fiercely.

Begin with Small, Manageable Steps

The art of transitioning is often best approached through gradual, small changes that compound over time. Start by incorporating one whole food meal into your day. Dedicate breakfast to be that meal where processed foods are swapped out for fresh fruits, whole grains, and seeds. As this becomes second nature, extend the practice to lunch, dinner, and finally snacks. Keep it simple and progressive—your palate will adjust, and soon, your cravings will too.

Involve Your Household

Your journey to whole food savoring is more delightful when shared. Engage your family in the process by involving them in meal planning and shopping. When children are part of the decision-making, they gain an understanding and appreciation for the foods on their plate. Encourage them to pick out a new fruit or vegetable during grocery runs—this involvement cultivates their interest and makes them more inclined to savor what they've chosen.

Simplify Your Pantry

A whole food kitchen is a canvas for your culinary creativity, so curate your pantry thoughtfully. Replace refined sugars with natural sweeteners like dates or honey, stock up on a variety of whole grains, and embrace the world of legumes. Detox your space of temptations that don't align with your whole food goals, but allow for a few transitional items as you ease into your new norm.

Learn the Label Lingo

Become a savvy shopper. Nutritional labels on packaging are a vignette of the product's journey before it reached the shelf. Learn to read and understand these prologues—the fewer the ingredients, the closer to whole food the product is. Look out for long, unpronounceable words that often signify added chemicals or preservatives. Keep it simple, in labels as in life.

Savor the Seasons

Whole foods possess an intrinsic wisdom, ripening in certain seasons for a reason. When you eat seasonally, you take in the nutrients best suited for the time of year. Seasonal produce is also often fresher, tastier, and more economical. Venture to local farmers' markets where the path from earth to table is short, and the produce's life force is still vibrant.

Craft a Love Affair with Cooking

If the kitchen has felt more like a place of obligation rather than inspiration, it's time to restore your relationship with it. Cooking should not be seen as a chore, but an art form and a way of self-expression. Start by mastering one new whole food recipe a week. Embrace the process of slicing, dicing, simmering, and sautéing as an act of love for yourself and those you feed. Cooking is the alchemy that transforms individual ingredients into a harmonious meal that sustains and thrills.

Cultivate Mindfulness

As you embark on this path, eat intentionally. Focus on the taste, texture, and joy in each bite. Turn meals into a meditative experience, where gratitude for the nourishing quality of whole foods takes center stage. Mindful eating naturally slows you down, making you more aware of your body's cues, and can even lead to better digestion and satisfaction with smaller portions.

Honor Your Journey

Some days, you'll revel in the fresh crunch of a just-picked apple, reveling in your whole food choices. Other days, the siren call of convenience food will echo in your ears. Recognize that transitions are bound to ebb and flow. Celebrate your successes, learn from slip-ups, and above all, be kind to yourself. This is a journey of discovery, not perfection.

Educate Yourself Continuously

Knowledge is power, and in the world of whole foods, it's also flavor, health, and pleasure. Read, research, and ask questions. The better you understand the nutritional value and potential health benefits of what you're eating, the more empowered you'll feel to make informed choices. Seek out sources that resonate with your newfound respect for food's wholesomeness, and let this knowledge become second nature.

Connect with Community

You are not alone in your quest for a healthier life through whole foods. Find groups, online forums, or local clubs that share your passion. Here, you can exchange ideas, encouragement, and recipes—a network of support that adds flavor to your journey.

Be the Catalyst for Change

Lastly, your commitment to whole foods can ripple outward, inspiring others. Share your experiences, serve whole food meals when you entertain, and gently spread the seed of wellness in your conversations.

In essence, shifting to whole food eating is akin to cultivating a garden. It takes time, patience, and care. But the bounty it yields—in the form of vibrant health, richer flavors, and a deeper appreciation for natural nourishment—is immeasurably fulfilling. Here's to the first step on this road less processed, where the meals are as abundant as nature intended and every bite resonates with life's purest flavors. Welcome to the wholesome revolution. Welcome to your new, whole foods life.

CHAPTER 2: BREAKFASTS TO START YOUR DAY RIGHT

2.1 ENERGIZING SMOOTHIES AND BOWLS

Moroccan mornings suffused with the songs of Tangier, Hawaiian sunrises that paint the waves, or the crisp air of a Vermont autumn—all these awakenings share a common thread: the need for a nourishing start. Our day's inception is more than routine; it's a sacrosanct moment where we cast the first stone across the waters of time that lie ahead.

Energizing smoothies and bowls are your allies in this daily genesis. They are the vibrant chorus to your morning's symphony, a blend of nature's own essence into concoctions that revive the spirit and fuel the body. Here, beneath the whirr of the blender, we find symphony in simplicity—a union of wholesome fruits, verdant greens, and robust seeds.

Imagine cradling a bowl imbued with the colors of the garden, each spoonful a testament to unrefined delight, or savoring a smoothie that whispers of berry fields and citrus groves. In these first meals of the day, we marry convenience with satisfaction—fuel for the body, pleasure for the palate, and peace for the soul. Let us lift the morning fog with these sustenance-laden creations, each a stepping stone toward vibrant health and unflagging energy.

GOLDEN TURMERIC MORNING ELIXIR

PREPARATION TIME: 5 min
COOKING TIME: none
SERVINGS: 2
M.OF COOKING: Blending
INGREDIENTS:
- 1 C. coconut milk
- 1 ripe banana
- ½ tsp turmeric powder
- ½ tsp grated fresh ginger
- 1 tsp chia seeds
- pinch of black pepper
- 1 Tbls raw honey
- ¼ tsp ground cinnamon

DIRECTIONS:
- Combine all ingredients in a high-speed blender
- Blend until smooth and creamy
- Pour into glasses and serve immediately

TIPS:
- Start your day with an anti-inflammatory boost with this elixir
- For a colder drink, use a frozen banana

N.V. : Calories: 180, Fat: 4g, Carbs: 35g, Protein: 2g, Sugar: 19g

AVOCADO MATCHA CHILLER

PREPARATION TIME: 5 min

COOKING TIME: none

SERVINGS: 1

M.OF COOKING: Blending

INGREDIENTS:

- ½ ripe avocado
- 1 tsp matcha green tea powder
- 1 C. unsweetened almond milk
- 1 Tbls raw honey
- ½ C. crushed ice
- 1 tsp hemp seeds
- 1 tsp flaxseed oil

DIRECTIONS:

- Scoop out the avocado into a blender
- Add the rest of the ingredients
- Blend on high until smooth
- Serve in a chilled glass

TIPS:

- Boost energy with matcha's slow-releasing caffeine
- Top with a sprinkle of hemp seeds for added texture

N.V. : Calories: 245, Fat: 19g, Carbs: 18g, Protein: 4g, Sugar: 12g

SPICED PEAR BREAKFAST QUINOA BOWL

PREPARATION TIME: 15 min

COOKING TIME: none

SERVINGS: 2

M.OF COOKING: Mixing

INGREDIENTS:

- 1 C. cooked quinoa
- 1 Bartlett pear, diced
- 1 Tbls chopped walnuts
- 1 Tbls pumpkin seeds
- 2 tsp pure maple syrup
- ½ tsp ground cinnamon
- pinch of nutmeg
- pinch of ground cloves
- ½ C. almond milk

DIRECTIONS:

- Combine cooked quinoa, diced pear, nuts, seeds, and spices in a bowl
- Drizzle with maple syrup
- Add almond milk just before serving

TIPS:

- Experiment with different nuts and seeds for varied flavors and textures
- Warm the almond milk for a cozier breakfast bowl

N.V. : Calories: 270, Fat: 6g, Carbs: 48g, Protein: 8g, Sugar: 15g

BEETROOT AND BERRY ENERGIZER

PREPARATION TIME: 7 min

COOKING TIME: none

SERVINGS: 2

M.OF COOKING: Blending

INGREDIENTS:

- 1 small beetroot, peeled and chopped
- ½ C. frozen mixed berries
- 1 ripe banana
- 1 C. coconut water
- 1 Tbls almond butter
- 1 tsp maca powder
- 1 Tbls lemon juice

DIRECTIONS:

- Place all ingredients in a high-speed blender
- Blend until smooth
- Serve immediately for maximum freshness

TIPS:

- The maca powder provides an energy lift perfect for mornings
- Save time by prepping and freezing beetroot in advance

N.V. : Calories: 150, Fat: 3g, Carbs: 30g, Protein: 4g, Sugar: 20g

SPIRULINA SUNRISE SMOOTHIE

PREPARATION TIME: 5 min

COOKING TIME: none

SERVINGS: 1

M.OF COOKING: Blending

INGREDIENTS:

- 1 C. orange juice
- 1 ripe banana
- ½ C. pineapple chunks
- 1 Tbls spirulina powder
- ½ C. spinach leaves
- ½ C. ice cubes

DIRECTIONS:

- Blend orange juice, banana, pineapple, spirulina, and spinach until smooth
- Add ice and pulse until frosty
- Pour into a tall glass and enjoy

TIPS:

- Spirulina adds a powerful nutrient punch to your morning routine
- If the taste is too strong, start with half a tablespoon and increase gradually

N.V. : Calories: 215, Fat: 1g, Carbs: 51g, Protein: 5g, Sugar: 35g

CHERRY ALMOND SUNRISE BOWL

PREPARATION TIME: 10 min

COOKING TIME: none

SERVINGS: 1

M.OF COOKING: Assembling

INGREDIENTS:

- 1 C. Greek yogurt, unsweetened
- ½ C. fresh cherries, pitted and halved
- 2 Tbls sliced almonds
- 1 Tbls dried goji berries
- 1 tsp raw honey
- dash of almond extract
- 1 Tbls chia seeds

DIRECTIONS:

- Layer Greek yogurt in a bowl
- Top with cherries, almonds, goji berries, and a drizzle of honey
- Finish with a dash of almond extract and sprinkle with chia seeds

TIPS:

- Pit the cherries the night before to streamline your morning
- Substitute with frozen cherries if fresh are not in season

N.V. : Calories: 290, Fat: 9g, Carbs: 36g, Protein: 18g, Sugar: 27g

GREEN TEA AND CITRUS TWIST

PREPARATION TIME: 5 min

COOKING TIME: none

SERVINGS: 1

M.OF COOKING: Blending

INGREDIENTS:

- 1 C. brewed green tea, cooled
- ½ C. cucumber, sliced
- ½ C. fresh spinach leaves
- 1 small orange, peeled
- 1 Tbls raw honey
- ¼ tsp grated ginger
- ½ C. ice

DIRECTIONS:

- Blend green tea, cucumber, spinach, orange, honey, and ginger until smooth
- Add ice and blend until frosty
- Pour into a glass and savor the zesty flavors

TIPS:

- Green tea offers an antioxidant boost for your day
- Make a larger batch of tea in advance and keep it in the fridge

N.V. : Calories: 120, Fat: 0g, Carbs: 30g, Protein: 2g, Sugar: 20g

2.2 HEARTY WHOLE GRAIN PORRIDGES AND PANCAKES

Welcome to the world where mornings are infused with the warmth of whole grains and the joy of fluffiness. Hearty whole grain porridges and pancakes aren't just your ticket to a satisfying breakfast; they are the sunrise on your day of well-being. Every spoonful is a promise of lasting energy, and each pancake is a canvas awaiting the bright colors of fresh fruits, natural syrups, and aromatic spices.

Embracing grains like quinoa, oats, and buckwheat invites an array of textures and flavors into your morning ritual. These grains aren't just nutrient powerhouses; they're historical staples, grounding us to a legacy of wellness. Revel in the simplicity of porridges that calm the morning rush, and delight in pancakes that turn your kitchen into a fragrant bakery. Let's start our day with intention and delight, plate by wholesome plate.

TRI-GRAIN APPLE CINNAMON PORRIDGE

PREPARATION TIME: 5 min.
COOKING TIME: 20 min.
SERVINGS: 4
M.OF COOKING: Stovetop
INGREDIENTS:
- 1 C. steel-cut oats
- 2 C. water
- 1 C. milk of choice
- 1 C. quinoa, rinsed
- 1/2 C. bulgur wheat
- 2 medium apples, peeled and diced
- 1/2 tsp ground cinnamon
- 1/4 tsp ground nutmeg
- 1/4 tsp sea salt
- 2 Tbls honey
- 1/4 C. chopped walnuts for garnish

DIRECTIONS:
- Combine steel-cut oats, water, and milk in a pot and bring to a boil
- Reduce heat to simmer and add quinoa and bulgur wheat, stirring frequently
- Once grains begin to soften, incorporate diced apples, cinnamon, nutmeg, and sea salt and continue to simmer
- Once everything is fully cooked and apples are tender, remove from heat and drizzle with honey before serving
- Garnish with chopped walnuts

TIPS:
- Stir in a dollop of almond butter for added creaminess and protein
- Top with a sprinkle of chia seeds for extra fiber
- Serve with a swirl of pure maple syrup for those who prefer a touch more sweetness

N.V. : Calories: 310, Fat: 8g, Carbs: 52g, Protein: 10g, Sugar: 15g

BUCKWHEAT BLUEBERRY LEMON PANCAKES

PREPARATION TIME: 15 min.

COOKING TIME: 20 min.

SERVINGS: 6

M.OF COOKING: Stovetop

INGREDIENTS:

- 1 1/2 C. buckwheat flour
- 2 tsp baking powder
- 1/4 tsp sea salt
- 1 Tbls lemon zest
- 1 C. blueberries, fresh
- 1 C. buttermilk
- 2 large eggs
- 1 Tbls lemon juice
- 2 Tbls unsalted butter, melted
- 1 Tbls honey
- Extra blueberries for serving
- Coconut oil for frying

DIRECTIONS:

- Whisk together buckwheat flour, baking powder, and sea salt in a bowl
- In a separate bowl, mix together buttermilk, eggs, lemon juice, melted butter, and honey
- Fold the wet ingredients into the dry ingredients until just combined and then gently fold in lemon zest and blueberries
- Heat a pan with coconut oil and ladle in portions of the batter, flipping pancakes once bubbles form and edges are golden brown
- Serve hot with additional blueberries on top

TIPS:

- Keep your batter lumpy for light and fluffy pancakes
- Use a non-stick pan or griddle to minimize the need for extra oil

- Garnish with a light dusting of powdered sugar for a decorative finish

N.V. : Calories: 220, Fat: 7g, Carbs: 33g, Protein: 6g, Sugar: 7g

SPICED TEFF PORRIDGE WITH DRIED FRUIT COMPOTE

PREPARATION TIME: 10 min.

COOKING TIME: 15 min.

SERVINGS: 4

M.OF COOKING: Stovetop

INGREDIENTS:

- 1 C. teff grain
- 3 C. water
- Pinch of sea salt
- 1/2 tsp ground cinnamon
- 1/4 tsp ground cardamom
- 1/4 tsp ground ginger
- 1/2 C. dried apricots, chopped
- 1/2 C. dried cranberries
- 1/4 C. raw honey
- 1/4 C. almond slivers for garnish

DIRECTIONS:

- Bring water to a boil with a pinch of sea salt and stir in teff grain, reducing the heat to a simmer
- Add cinnamon, cardamom, and ginger, continuing to stir occasionally to prevent sticking
- In a separate pan, heat dried apricots and cranberries with a splash of water until they become plump and create a compote
- Once teff is cooked through, stir in honey for natural sweetness
- Serve the porridge topped with the warm fruit compote and garnish with almond slivers

TIPS:

- For an extra burst of flavor, sauté the dried fruits with a splash of orange juice instead of water
- Consider soaking teff overnight to reduce cooking time
- Toast the almond slivers for added crunch and a nuttier flavor

N.V. : Calories: 290, Fat: 3g, Carbs: 62g, Protein: 7g, Sugar: 29g

MILLET AND CHIA SEED PANCAKES

PREPARATION TIME: 10 min.

COOKING TIME: 15 min.

SERVINGS: 4

M.OF COOKING: Stovetop

INGREDIENTS:
- 1 C. millet flour
- 2 Tbls chia seeds
- 1 Tbls flaxseed meal
- 2 tsp baking powder
- Pinch of sea salt
- 1 C. almond milk
- 1 Tbls apple cider vinegar
- 1 large egg
- 1 Tbls coconut oil, melted plus more for frying
- 1 Tbls maple syrup

DIRECTIONS:
- In a bowl, mix together millet flour, chia seeds, flaxseed meal, baking powder, and sea salt
- In a separate bowl, combine almond milk and apple cider vinegar, allowing to sit for 5 min. to create "buttermilk"
- Whisk egg into "buttermilk" mixture and add in melted coconut oil and maple syrup
- Blend the wet ingredients into the dry until you have a smooth batter

- Heat a pan with coconut oil and pour in batter to form pancakes, cooking until bubbles appear and edges crisp
- Flip pancakes and cook until golden brown on both sides

TIPS:
- Use room temperature ingredients to prevent the coconut oil from solidifying when mixed
- For extra fluffiness, let the batter rest for 5 minutes before cooking
- Serve with a dollop of Greek yogurt for added protein and creaminess

N.V. : Calories: 180, Fat: 8g, Carbs: 23g, Protein: 5g, Sugar: 3g

AMARANTH PUMPKIN PORRIDGE

PREPARATION TIME: 10 min.

COOKING TIME: 25 min.

SERVINGS: 4

M.OF COOKING: Stovetop

INGREDIENTS:
- 1 C. amaranth
- 2 C. water
- 1 C. pumpkin puree
- 1 tsp vanilla extract
- 1/2 tsp ground cinnamon
- 1/4 tsp ground nutmeg
- 1/4 tsp ground cloves
- 3 Tbls maple syrup
- 2 Tbls pumpkin seeds for garnish

DIRECTIONS:
- Rinse amaranth and combine with water in a saucepan, bringing to a boil before reducing to a simmer
- Stir in pumpkin puree, vanilla extract, cinnamon, nutmeg, and cloves, cooking until amaranth is tender and porridge is thick
- Remove from heat and sweeten with maple syrup

- Serve hot, sprinkled with pumpkin seeds on top

TIPS:

- To enhance the porridge's creaminess, add a splash of coconut milk during the last few minutes of cooking
- Garnish with a few grates of fresh nutmeg for an aromatic finish
- Incorporate a tablespoon of collagen powder for additional health benefits

N.V. : Calories: 260, Fat: 4g, Carbs: 49g, Protein: 7g, Sugar: 11g

WILD RICE APPLE PANCAKES WITH CINNAMON

PREPARATION TIME: 15 min.

COOKING TIME: 20 min.

SERVINGS: 6

M.OF COOKING: Stovetop

INGREDIENTS:

- 1 C. cooked wild rice
- 1 C. whole wheat flour
- 1 1/2 tsp baking powder
- 1/2 tsp ground cinnamon
- 1/4 tsp salt
- 1 C. milk of choice
- 1 Tbls maple syrup
- 1 large egg
- 1 medium apple, grated
- Coconut oil for cooking

DIRECTIONS:

- Mix together cooked wild rice, whole wheat flour, baking powder, ground cinnamon, and salt in a bowl
- In another bowl, whisk together milk, maple syrup, and egg
- Gently fold in the grated apple and then combine the wet and dry ingredients

- Heat a skillet with coconut oil and pour batter to form pancakes, cooking until each side is golden brown and fully set

TIPS:

- Serve with extra apple slices on the side for added crunch and freshness
- Experiment with pear instead of apple for a different flavor profile
- Incorporate a spoonful of natural yogurt into the batter for a tangier taste

N.V. : Calories: 197, Fat: 3g, Carbs: 37g, Protein: 6g, Sugar: 7g

SORGHUM AND ALMOND BUTTER PORRIDGE

PREPARATION TIME: 5 min.

COOKING TIME: 30 min.

SERVINGS: 4

M.OF COOKING: Stovetop

INGREDIENTS:

- 1 C. whole grain sorghum
- 4 C. water
- 1/4 tsp sea salt
- 2 Tbls almond butter
- 1 banana, sliced
- 1 Tbls chia seeds
- 1/4 C. almond milk
- 1 tsp vanilla extract
- 1 Tbls honey
- Sliced almonds and banana for garnish

DIRECTIONS:

- Rinse sorghum and combine with water and sea salt in a pot, bringing to a boil and then reducing to simmer, cooking until tender
- Stir in almond butter, banana slices, chia seeds, almond milk, and vanilla extract until well combined and creamy

- Drizzle with honey before serving and garnish with sliced almonds and additional banana slices

TIPS:

- Soak sorghum overnight to cut down on cooking time

- Stir occasionally while cooking to prevent sticking and to encourage creaminess
- Add a pinch of cinnamon or cocoa powder for a flavor twist

N.V. : Calories: 335, Fat: 9g, Carbs: 59g, Protein: 8g, Sugar: 10g

2.3 PROTEIN-PACKED EGG DISHES

Eggs, nature's multivitamin, are a morning staple for a reason. They are versatile, rich in protein, and a golden thread in the tapestry of nourishing breakfast options. In this section, we'll explore egg dishes that go beyond the traditional scramble. We're talking about omelets filled with garden-fresh vegetables, poached parcels of delight sitting atop whole-grain toasts, and frittatas bursting with the flavors of seasonal produce. These protein-packed creations will energize your mornings with their healthful ingredients and the endless possibilities they present. Each recipe is designed to be accessible for busy mornings yet impressive enough for a leisurely brunch. Let's crack into the culinary potential of eggs and elevate your breakfast to a celebration of whole food goodness.

SHAKSHUKA WITH SWISS CHARD

PREPARATION TIME: 15 min
COOKING TIME: 30 min
SERVINGS: 4
M.OF COOKING: Stovetop
INGREDIENTS:
- 1 Tbls extra virgin olive oil
- 1 medium onion, thinly sliced
- 2 garlic cloves, minced
- 1 tsp ground cumin
- ½ tsp smoked paprika
- ¼ tsp cayenne pepper
- 1 lb. Swiss chard, stems removed and leaves chopped
- 1 28-oz can whole peeled tomatoes, crushed by hand
- 4 large free-range eggs
- Salt and fresh ground black pepper to taste
- Fresh cilantro, chopped for garnish
- Whole grain bread for serving

DIRECTIONS:
- Heat oil in a skillet over medium heat
- Add onion and garlic, cook until translucent
- Stir in spices and cook for another minute
- Add Swiss chard, cook until wilted
- Pour in tomatoes, season with salt and pepper, and simmer for 15 min
- Create wells in the sauce and crack an egg into each
- Cover and cook until eggs are set to desired doneness
- Garnish with cilantro and serve with bread

TIPS:
- Bake in the sauce longer for firmer eggs
- Serve with a dollop of plain yogurt for extra creaminess
- Swap out chard for kale or spinach for variety

N.V. : Calories: 210, Fat: 11g, Carbs: 18g, Protein: 12g, Sugar: 10g

HERB-INFUSED MUSHROOM OMELETTE

PREPARATION TIME: 10 min
COOKING TIME: 10 min
SERVINGS: 2
M.OF COOKING: Stovetop
INGREDIENTS:
- 4 large free-range eggs
- 1 Tbls water
- ¼ tsp sea salt
- Ground black pepper to taste
- 1 Tbls unsalted grass-fed butter

- ½ C. shiitake mushrooms, thinly sliced
- 1 Tbls fresh thyme leaves
- 1 Tbls chervil, chopped
- 1 Tbls parsley, chopped
- ¼ C. goat cheese, crumbled

DIRECTIONS:
- Whisk eggs, water, salt, and pepper together
- In a non-stick skillet, melt butter over medium heat
- Saute shiitake mushrooms until tender
- Pour egg mixture over mushrooms, sprinkle with herbs
- Cook without stirring until edges begin to set
- Add goat cheese over half the omelette
- Fold over and cook to desired consistency

TIPS:
- Try with different mushroom varieties for distinct flavors
- Add a splash of truffle oil for an indulgent twist
- Use feta cheese instead of goat cheese for a tangier taste

N.V. : Calories: 320, Fat: 25g, Carbs: 4g, Protein: 20g, Sugar: 2g

SUN-DRIED TOMATO FRITTATA SQUARES

PREPARATION TIME: 15 min

COOKING TIME: 25 min

SERVINGS: 6

M.OF COOKING: Oven

INGREDIENTS:
- 10 large free-range eggs
- ½ C. full-fat milk
- 1 C. sun-dried tomatoes, julienned
- ½ C. raw spinach, chopped
- 1 small red onion, finely diced
- ⅓ C. Kalamata olives, pitted and sliced
- 2 oz. feta cheese, crumbled

- 2 Tbls fresh basil, chopped
- Sea salt and black pepper to taste
- 1 Tbls extra virgin olive oil

DIRECTIONS:
- Preheat oven to 350°F (175°C)
- Whisk together eggs, milk, salt, and pepper
- In a 9x13 inch baking dish, sauté red onion in olive oil until soft
- Add spinach, sun-dried tomatoes, olives, and pour over egg mixture
- Scatter feta and basil on top
- Bake until set and golden, about 25 min.
- Cut into squares to serve

TIPS:
- Experiment with different herbs like oregano or thyme for varied flavors
- Serve with a side of arugula salad for a complete meal
- Perfect for meal prep: store individual squares for a quick breakfast option

N.V. : Calories: 280, Fat: 20g, Carbs: 8g, Protein: 16g, Sugar: 5g

SPICY KIMCHI SCRAMBLED EGGS

PREPARATION TIME: 5 min

COOKING TIME: 10 min

SERVINGS: 2

M.OF COOKING: Stovetop

INGREDIENTS:
- 4 large free-range eggs
- 1 Tbls coconut oil
- 1 Tbls tamari or coconut aminos
- ½ C. kimchi, roughly chopped
- 2 scallions, thinly sliced
- ¼ tsp crushed red pepper flakes
- Toasted sesame seeds for garnish
- Sea salt to taste

DIRECTIONS:

- Heat coconut oil in a skillet on medium heat
- Add kimchi and scallions, sauté for 2-3 min
- Beat eggs with tamari and a pinch of salt
- Pour into skillet, sprinkle with red pepper flakes
- Scramble eggs until just set
- Garnish with toasted sesame seeds to serve

TIPS:

- Incorporate freshly minced garlic for an additional flavor kick
- Serve over steamed brown rice for a heartier dish
- Add a splash of sesame oil for a nutty finish

N.V. : Calories: 220, Fat: 17g, Carbs: 3g, Protein: 14g, Sugar: 2g

SAVORY SPINACH AND FETA FRITTATA

PREPARATION TIME: 10 min.

COOKING TIME: 20 min.

SERVINGS: 6

M.OF COOKING: Baked

INGREDIENTS:

- 6 large eggs
- 1 C. fresh spinach, chopped
- ½ C. feta cheese, crumbled
- ¼ C. red onion, finely sliced
- 2 Tbls extra virgin olive oil
- ½ tsp garlic powder
- 1 Tbls fresh dill, chopped
- Salt and pepper to taste

DIRECTIONS:

- Preheat oven to 375°F (190°C)
- In a bowl, whisk eggs, garlic powder, dill, salt, and pepper
- Heat olive oil in an oven-safe skillet over medium heat and sauté red onion until soft

- Add spinach and wilt slightly
- Pour the egg mixture over the veggies and sprinkle feta cheese on top
- Transfer the skillet to the oven and bake until eggs are set

TIPS:

- Use a cast iron skillet for even cooking and easy transfer from stovetop to oven
- Frittata can be served hot or at room temperature
- Garnish with fresh dill for an additional burst of flavor

N.V. : Calories: 180, Fat: 14g, Carbs: 3g, Protein: 11g, Sugar: 2g

KIMCHI AND LEEK OMELETTE

PREPARATION TIME: 5 min.

COOKING TIME: 8 min.

SERVINGS: 2

M.OF COOKING: Pan-fried

INGREDIENTS:

- 4 large eggs
- ½ C. kimchi, chopped
- 1 small leek, cleaned and thinly sliced
- 1 Tbls sesame oil
- 1 tsp sesame seeds
- 1 Tbls tamari or soy sauce
- 1 tsp gochugaru (Korean chili flakes)
- Salt to taste

DIRECTIONS:

- Whisk eggs, tamari, gochugaru, and salt
- Heat sesame oil in a non-stick frying pan over medium heat
- Sauté leeks until tender
- Add kimchi and stir for a minute
- Pour the egg mixture over the leek and kimchi
- Cook until edges firm up, then gently fold the omelette in half
- Continue to cook until eggs are fully set

TIPS:

- Serve with a sprinkle of sesame seeds on top for a nutty flavor
- Add green onions as a garnish for extra zest
- Use well-fermented kimchi for a deeper flavor

N.V. : Calories: 235, Fat: 18g, Carbs: 4g, Protein: 14g, Sugar: 3g

HERBED SHIRRED EGGS WITH GRUYÈRE

PREPARATION TIME: 15 min.

COOKING TIME: 12 min.

SERVINGS: 4

M.OF COOKING: Baked

INGREDIENTS:

- 8 large eggs
- ½ C. Gruyère cheese, grated
- 2 Tbls heavy cream
- 1 Tbls fresh thyme, chopped
- 1 Tbls fresh chives, chopped
- 2 Tbls unsalted butter
- Salt and pepper to taste

DIRECTIONS:

- Preheat oven to 375°F (190°C)
- Generously butter ramekins
- In each ramekin, crack two eggs and add a Tbls of cream
- Sprinkle with salt, pepper, thyme, and chives
- Top with grated Gruyère
- Place ramekins in a baking dish and fill dish with boiling water halfway up the sides of ramekins
- Bake until whites are set but yolks are still runny

TIPS:

- Recommend serving with crusty whole grain bread
- Sharp cheddar can be substituted for Gruyère for a different flavor profile
- Grate the cheese freshly to ensure the best melt

N.V. : Calories: 245, Fat: 19g, Carbs: 1g, Protein: 17g, Sugar: 0.5g

CHAPTER 3: NUTRITIOUS AND FILLING LUNCHES

3.1 VIBRANT SALADS WITH HOMEMADE DRESSINGS

Welcome to the world where the humble salad is anything but a side note. In this section, we'll whisk you away from mundane mixed greens into a universe of vibrant salads, each bursting with color, texture, and flavor, topped off with the magic touch of homemade dressings. Imagine a midday meal that refreshes your palate while replenishing your energy—gleaming ruby tomatoes, crisp emerald spinach, and golden-roasted nuts, all coming together in a symphony of natural wholesomeness.

Gone are the days of stark lettuce and dreary cubed carrots. We invite you to embrace the adventure of crafting salads that stand as a testament to your creativity and your body's needs. From the zesty allure of a citrus vinaigrette to the creamy embrace of an avocado dressing, these concoctions are not just drizzles, but heartfelt expressions of homemade love. Who said lunches have to be sleepy? Let's toss that idea out and bowl over family and friends with dishes that invigorate and sustain you through your bustling day. Get ready to mix, dress, and feast to your heart's content!

CRISPY RAINBOW KALE SALAD WITH MISO TAHINI DRESSING

PREPARATION TIME: 15 min
COOKING TIME: none
SERVINGS: 4
M.OF COOKING: Raw Assembly
INGREDIENTS:

- 1 bunch Lacinato kale, ribs removed, leaves thinly sliced
  - 1 medium beet, peeled and julienned
  - 1 large carrot, peeled and ribboned
  - 1/2 red bell pepper, thinly sliced
  - 1/4 red onion, thinly sliced
  - 1/4 C. raw sunflower seeds
  - 1/4 C. dried cranberries
  - For Dressing: 2 Tbls tahini
  - 1 Tbls apple cider vinegar
  - 1 Tbls white miso
  - 1 Tbls warm water
  - 1 tsp pure maple syrup
  - 1 clove garlic, minced

DIRECTIONS:

- In a large bowl, combine all salad ingredients

35

- In a small bowl, whisk together the dressing ingredients until smooth
- Pour dressing over the salad and toss to coat evenly

TIPS:

- Massage kale with a pinch of salt to soften the leaves
- Beet can be roasted if preferred for a sweeter taste
- Sunflower seeds can be toasted for an added crunch

N.V. : Calories: 180, Fat: 11g, Carbs: 19g, Protein: 5g, Sugar: 7g

AVOCADO & GRAPEFRUIT QUINOA SALAD WITH ADOBO LIME DRESSING

PREPARATION TIME: 20 min

COOKING TIME: none

SERVINGS: 2

M.OF COOKING: Raw Assembly

INGREDIENTS:

- 1 C. cooked quinoa, chilled
- 1 large avocado, diced
- 1 ruby red grapefruit, segments removed
- 1/2 C. arugula
- 2 Tbls sliced almonds
- For Dressing: 2 Tbls fresh lime juice
- 1 Tbls extra virgin olive oil
- 1 tsp adobo seasoning
- 1/2 tsp honey
- Salt and pepper to taste

DIRECTIONS:

- In a serving bowl, mix the quinoa, avocado, grapefruit segments, and arugula
- In a separate container, combine all dressing ingredients and whisk until well-blended
- Drizzle dressing over the salad and sprinkle with sliced almonds

TIPS:

- Quinoa can be replaced with amaranth for a nuttier flavor
- Add thinly sliced fennel for an aromatic twist
- Dressing can be emulsified in a blender for a creamier texture

N.V. : Calories: 310, Fat: 15g, Carbs: 40g, Protein: 8g, Sugar: 8g

SPELT BERRY SALAD WITH ROASTED POBLANO VINAIGRETTE

PREPARATION TIME: 25 min

COOKING TIME: none

SERVINGS: 4

M.OF COOKING: Raw Assembly

INGREDIENTS:

- 2 C. cooked spelt berries
- 1 large tomato, diced
- 1 cucumber, seeded and diced
- 1/4 C. fresh cilantro, chopped
- 1/4 C. red onion, finely chopped
- For Dressing: 2 Tbls roasted poblano pepper, skin removed, puréed
- 3 Tbls extra virgin olive oil
- 1 Tbls red wine vinegar
- 1 clove garlic, minced
- 1/2 tsp ground cumin
- Salt and pepper to taste

DIRECTIONS:

- Combine spelt berries, tomato, cucumber, cilantro, and red onion in a bowl
- For the dressing, whisk all ingredients until well combined
- Pour over the spelt berry mixture and toss well

TIPS:

- Spelt berries can be soaked overnight to reduce cooking time
- Roast additional poblano peppers and freeze for future use

• Add a pinch of smoked paprika to the dressing for extra depth

N.V. : Calories: 210, Fat: 8g, Carbs: 32g, Protein: 6g, Sugar: 2g

SHAVED BRUSSELS SPROUT CAESAR WITH CASHEW-PARM CRISPS

PREPARATION TIME: 30 min

COOKING TIME: none

SERVINGS: 2

M.OF COOKING: Raw Assembly

INGREDIENTS:

• 3 C. Brussels sprouts, trimmed and thinly sliced
• 1/4 C. cashew nuts, soaked and drained
• 3 Tbls nutritional yeast
• 1 Tbls lemon juice
• For Crisps: 1/4 C. cashew nuts
• 2 Tbls nutritional yeast
• For Dressing: 2 Tbls Greek yogurt
• 1 Tbls lemon juice
• 1 tsp Dijon mustard
• 1 small clove garlic, minced
• Salt and pepper to taste
• Water as needed

DIRECTIONS:

• For the crisps, pulse cashews and nutritional yeast in a food processor until crumbly and bake at 350°F (175°C) until golden
• Mix Brussels sprouts with cashews, nutritional yeast, and lemon juice in a bowl
• In a small bowl, prepare the dressing by whisking together Greek yogurt, lemon juice, Dijon mustard, garlic, and seasoning, thinning with water as needed
• Toss the salad with the dressing and top with cashew-parm crisps

TIPS:

• Cashews for crisps can be replaced with almonds or breadcrumbs for variety
• Dressing can be made vegan with silken tofu substitution
• Lemon zest can be added for extra zing

N.V. : Calories: 240, Fat: 16g, Carbs: 18g, Protein: 9g, Sugar: 3g

WARM LENTIL SALAD WITH CHARRED LEEKS VINAIGRETTE

PREPARATION TIME: 25 min

COOKING TIME: 5 min

SERVINGS: 4

M.OF COOKING: Grilling/Sautéing

INGREDIENTS:

• 2 C. green lentils, cooked
• 2 medium leeks, cleaned and halved lengthwise
• 1 C. cherry tomatoes, halved
• 1/4 C. fresh parsley, chopped
• For Dressing: 3 Tbls extra virgin olive oil
• 2 Tbls balsamic vinegar
• 1 Tbls Dijon mustard
• 1 Tbls honey
• Salt and pepper to taste

DIRECTIONS:

• Grill leeks until charred, then finely chop
• Combine lentils, tomatoes, parsley, and chopped leeks in a serving bowl
• Whisk together the dressing ingredients and pour over the salad, toss to combine

TIPS:

• Lentils can be cooked in vegetable broth for added flavor
• Add some crumbled goat cheese for a tangy touch
• Cherry tomatoes can be quickly grilled for a smoky sweetness

N.V. : Calories: 250, Fat: 9g, Carbs: 33g, Protein: 12g, Sugar: 6g

KALEIDOSCOPE QUINOA SALAD

PREPARATION TIME: 15 min

COOKING TIME: none

SERVINGS: 4

M. OF COOKING: No Cooking

INGREDIENTS:

- 1 C. tri-color quinoa, cooked and cooled
- 1 small red onion, finely sliced
- 1 C. cherry tomatoes, halved
- 1 yellow bell pepper, diced
- 1 C. cucumber, diced
- 1 Avocado, diced
- 1/4 C. fresh cilantro, chopped
- 1/4 C. extra-virgin olive oil
- 2 Tbls apple cider vinegar
- Juice of 1 lemon
- 1 garlic clove, minced
- Salt and pepper to taste

DIRECTIONS:

- Combine quinoa, red onion, cherry tomatoes, bell pepper, cucumber, avocado, and cilantro in a large bowl
- In a separate bowl, whisk together olive oil, apple cider vinegar, lemon juice, minced garlic, salt, and pepper to create the dressing
- Pour dressing over salad and gently toss to coat evenly

TIPS:

- Serve immediately or let the salad marinate for an hour for enhanced flavors
- Add grilled chicken or tofu for a protein boost
- This salad can be stored in an airtight container in the fridge for up to 2 days

N.V. : Calories: 348, Fat: 18g, Carbs: 42g, Protein: 8g, Sugar: 5g

RUBY BEETROOT & GOAT CHEESE TANGLE

PREPARATION TIME: 20 min.

COOKING TIME: none

SERVINGS: 4

M. OF COOKING: No Cooking

INGREDIENTS:

- 2 medium beetroots, peeled and julienned
- 3 C. arugula leaves
- 1/2 C. goat cheese, crumbled
- 1/4 C. walnuts, toasted and chopped
- 3 Tbls extra-virgin olive oil
- 1 Tbls balsamic reduction
- 2 tsp honey
- 1 tsp Dijon mustard
- Salt and pepper to taste

DIRECTIONS:

- Toss julienned beetroots and arugula in a salad bowl
- Gently fold in crumbled goat cheese and toasted walnuts
- In a small bowl, whisk together olive oil, balsamic reduction, honey, Dijon mustard, salt, and pepper to craft the dressing
- Drizzle dressing over the salad just before serving

TIPS:

- Enhance the complexity of flavors by adding fresh herbs like mint or basil
- For a nuttier essence, substitute walnuts with toasted pine nuts
- Balsamic reduction can be made by simmering balsamic vinegar until it thickens and becomes sweeter

N.V. : Calories: 220, Fat: 16g, Carbs: 13g, Protein: 7g, Sugar: 9g

3.2 WHOLESOME SOUPS AND STEWS

In the heartwarming embrace of a bowl of soup or stew lies the gentle power to transform your midday meal into a nourishing escape. Each spoonful is a symphony of flavors that not only satisfies hunger but also infuses your body with an array of healthful nutrients. In the hustle of daily life, these liquid treasures offer a comforting respite, grounding us in the moment and in the goodness of what nature provides.

Imagine the kitchen filled with the aromatic whispers of simmering vegetables and herbs, the steam carrying tales of tradition and well-being. Here, we will explore a collection of soups and stews that are as kind to your schedule as they are to your body. Crafted with love and simplicity, these recipes are your steadfast allies in a quest for a balanced, vibrant lunchtime reprieve. Whether ladled from a family-sized pot or enjoyed alone with a reflective pause, these dishes promise to be a cornerstone of your whole food journey, one heartwarming bowl at a time.

RUSTIC WHITE BEAN AND FENNEL SOUP

PREPARATION TIME: 15 min.

COOKING TIME: 35 min.

SERVINGS: 4

M.OF COOKING: Stovetop

INGREDIENTS:

- 2 Tbls extra virgin olive oil
- 1 bulb fennel, thinly sliced
- 1 onion, diced
- 2 cloves garlic, minced
- 1 tsp dried thyme
- 1 bay leaf
- 4 C. vegetable broth
- 1 C. white beans, cooked
- 1 C. kale, de-stemmed and torn
- Salt to taste
- Freshly ground black pepper to taste

DIRECTIONS:

- Heat olive oil in a soup pot over medium heat
- Add fennel and onion, cooking until translucent
- Stir in garlic, thyme, and bay leaf, cooking for another minute
- Pour in vegetable broth and bring to a boil
- Add white beans and let simmer for 30 min.
- Add kale in the last 5 min. of cooking
- Season with salt and pepper
- Remove bay leaf before serving

TIPS:

- Serve with a sprinkle of fennel fronds for garnish
- A squeeze of lemon juice can add a refreshing twist
- Pair with crusty whole grain bread for a hearty meal

N.V. : Calories: 208, Fat: 5g, Carbs: 30g, Protein: 10g, Sugar: 3g

MOROCCAN LENTIL AND CHICKPEA STEW

PREPARATION TIME: 20 min.

COOKING TIME: 55 min.

SERVINGS: 6

M.OF COOKING: Stovetop

INGREDIENTS:

- 1 Tbls coconut oil
- 2 carrots, diced
- 1 onion, diced

- 3 cloves garlic, minced
- 1 tsp ground cumin
- 1 tsp ground coriander
- ½ tsp ground cinnamon
- ¼ tsp cayenne pepper
- 1 C. green lentils
- 1 qt. vegetable stock
- 1 14.5-oz. can diced tomatoes
- 1 15-oz. can chickpeas, drained and rinsed
- 1 C. spinach, chopped
- 1 Tbls honey
- Salt and pepper to taste

DIRECTIONS:

- In a large pot, heat coconut oil over medium heat
- Sauté carrots and onion until softened
- Add garlic and spices, stirring for about 1 min.
- Stir in lentils, vegetable stock, and tomatoes and bring to a boil
- Reduce heat, cover, and simmer for 45 min. or until lentils are tender
- Stir in chickpeas, spinach, and honey, heating through
- Season with salt and pepper

TIPS:

- Top with a dollop of natural yogurt and a sprinkle of fresh cilantro for added flavor and texture
- Serve with a side of whole grain flatbread

N.V. : Calories: 276, Fat: 4g, Carbs: 49g, Protein: 17g, Sugar: 9g

THAI COCONUT CURRY BUTTERNUT SQUASH SOUP

PREPARATION TIME: 15 min.

COOKING TIME: 30 min.

SERVINGS: 4

M.OF COOKING: Stovetop

INGREDIENTS:

- 1 Tbls coconut oil
- 1 small onion, chopped
- 2 cloves garlic, minced
- 2 Tbls red curry paste
- 1 medium butternut squash, peeled and cubed
- 1 14-oz. can coconut milk
- 2 C. vegetable broth
- 1 Tbls maple syrup
- 1 tsp sea salt
- 1 lime, juiced
- Fresh cilantro for garnish

DIRECTIONS:

- In a large pot, melt coconut oil over medium heat
- Add onion and garlic and sauté until translucent
- Stir in red curry paste
- Add butternut squash and sauté for a few minutes
- Pour in coconut milk and vegetable broth
- Bring to a low boil, then simmer until squash is tender
- Puree soup with an immersion blender until smooth
- Stir in maple syrup, sea salt, and lime juice

TIPS:

- Garnish with fresh cilantro and a drizzle of coconut milk
- For extra heat, top with sliced red chili peppers
- Serve with a side of jasmine rice for a complete meal

N.V. : Calories: 255, Fat: 19g, Carbs: 22g, Protein: 3g, Sugar: 6g

SMOKEY POTATO AND LEEK STEW

PREPARATION TIME: 10 min.

COOKING TIME: 40 min.

SERVINGS: 6

M.OF COOKING: Stovetop

INGREDIENTS:

- 2 Tbls olive oil
- 3 large leeks, white and light green parts only, chopped
- 2 cloves garlic, minced
- 2 tbsps smoked paprika
- 5 large potatoes, peeled and diced
- 6 C. vegetable broth
- Salt to taste
- Freshly ground black pepper to taste
- Chopped chives for serving

DIRECTIONS:

- Warm olive oil in a large pot over medium heat
- Add leeks and cook until soft
- Stir in garlic and smoked paprika and cook for 1 min.
- Add potatoes and vegetable broth and bring to a simmer
- Cook until potatoes are tender, about 30 min.
- Mash some of the potatoes to thicken the stew
- Season with salt and pepper

TIPS:

- Sprinkle with chopped chives for added flavor and a pop of color
- Serve with whole grain sourdough bread for dunking
- A pinch of smoked sea salt enhances the smoky flavor even further

N.V. : Calories: 210, Fat: 4.5g, Carbs: 39g, Protein: 4g, Sugar: 3g

ROASTED BUTTERNUT SQUASH AND CARROT BISQUE

PREPARATION TIME: 20 min.

COOKING TIME: 40 min.

SERVINGS: 6

M.OF COOKING: Stovetop

INGREDIENTS:

- 1 medium butternut squash, peeled, seeded, and cubed
- 3 large carrots, peeled and chopped
- 1 yellow onion, diced
- 3 cloves garlic, minced
- 4 C. vegetable stock
- 1 C. light coconut milk
- 2 Tbls extra virgin olive oil
- 1 tsp ground cinnamon
- ½ tsp ground nutmeg
- Sea salt and freshly-ground pepper to taste
- Fresh parsley, chopped, for garnish

DIRECTIONS:

- Preheat a soup pot over medium heat and add olive oil
- Saute onion until translucent
- Add garlic and cook until fragrant
- Toss in the butternut squash, carrots, cinnamon, nutmeg, salt, and pepper, cooking for a few minutes
- Pour in the vegetable stock, bring to a boil, then cover and simmer for 30 min. or until vegetables are tender
- Blend the mixture using an immersion blender until smooth
- Stir in the coconut milk and heat through
- Serve garnished with fresh parsley

TIPS:

- Roast squash and carrots in a 400°F (204°C) oven before adding to the pot for added depth of flavor

- Top with toasted pumpkin seeds for a crunchy texture
- Use freshly grated nutmeg for the most potent flavor

N.V. : Calories: 172, Fat: 7g, Carbs: 27g, Protein: 2g, Sugar: 6g

SPICY LENTIL AND KALE STEW

PREPARATION TIME: 15 min.

COOKING TIME: 35 min.

SERVINGS: 4

M.OF COOKING: Stovetop

INGREDIENTS:
- 1 C. green lentils, rinsed
- 1 bunch kale, stemmed and chopped
- 1 can (15 oz.) diced tomatoes
- 4 C. low sodium vegetable broth
- 1 yellow onion, chopped
- 2 carrots, peeled and diced
- 2 Tbls tomato paste
- 3 Tbls extra virgin olive oil
- 2 tsp cumin seeds
- 1 tsp smoked paprika
- 1 tsp chili flakes
- Sea salt and freshly-ground pepper to taste
- Lemon wedges for serving

DIRECTIONS:
- Heat oil in a large pot on medium heat
- Add cumin seeds and toast until fragrant
- Saute onion and carrots until soft
- Stir in tomato paste, smoked paprika, chili flakes, salt, and pepper
- Add diced tomatoes and cook for 5 min.
- Pour in lentils and vegetable broth, bring to a simmer, cover, and cook for 25 min. or until lentils are cooked
- Add kale and simmer until wilted
- Serve hot with a squeeze of lemon

TIPS:

- Serve with a dollop of Greek yogurt to balance the spices
- Substitute kale with swiss chard or spinach for variation
- Add a piece of Parmesan rind while simmering for added umami depth

N.V. : Calories: 324, Fat: 10g, Carbs: 44g, Protein: 17g, Sugar: 7g

HEARTY MUSHROOM AND BARLEY SOUP

PREPARATION TIME: 10 min.

COOKING TIME: 1 hr.

SERVINGS: 6

M.OF COOKING: Stovetop

INGREDIENTS:
- 1 C. pearl barley
- 1 lb. mixed wild mushrooms, roughly chopped
- 1 leek, white and light green parts only, thinly sliced
- 2 Tbls unsalted butter
- 6 C. mushroom or vegetable broth
- 2 Tbls dill, chopped
- 1 Tbls tamari or soy sauce
- 1 Tbls apple cider vinegar
- 2 bay leaves
- Sea salt and freshly-ground pepper to taste

DIRECTIONS:
- Melt butter in a heavy-bottomed soup pot over medium heat
- Saute leek until softened
- Add mushrooms and cook until all moisture has evaporated and they begin to brown
- Stir in barley, bay leaves, and broth, bring to a boil, then reduce heat to simmer for about 50 min. or until the barley is tender
- Remove bay leaves

- Add tamari, vinegar, and dill, adjusting seasoning to taste
- Simmer for an additional 10 min.

TIPS:
- Use a combination of shiitake, cremini, and oyster mushrooms for the best flavor complexity

- If desired, finish with a splash of truffle oil for an earthy aroma
- For a creamier texture, stir in a few tablespoons of Greek yogurt before serving

N.V. : Calories: 225, Fat: 4g, Carbs: 41g, Protein: 6g, Sugar: 5g

3.3 LIGHT AND FLAVORFUL WRAPS AND SANDWICHES

In our bustling world, lunch often becomes an afterthought—yet, it holds the power to rejuvenate our day. Imagine unwrapping a bundle of joy: a wrap, light yet satisfying, or a sandwich packed with colors and textures as vibrant as a garden in bloom. In this subchapter, we celebrate the art of crafting wraps and sandwiches that combine convenience with culinary delight.

Gone are the days of dull, soggy sandwiches. Instead, we'll explore the alchemy of whole grains, lean proteins, and a rainbow of vegetables wrapped in a tender embrace. Each recipe whispers a promise: to turn your midday meals into moments of nourishment and pleasure without sacrifice. Whether you're yearning for a zesty, lean turkey wrap kissed by herbs or a rustic sandwich with layers of roasted vegetables, these creations will not only satisfy your hunger but will also invite you to savor each bite as an act of self-love and care. Let's cherish our lunch break as a feast for the senses, and fuel our afternoons with grace and vitality.

CURRIED CHICKPEA SALAD WRAP

PREPARATION TIME: 15 min

COOKING TIME: none

SERVINGS: 4

M.OF COOKING: No Cooking

INGREDIENTS:
- 2 C. canned chickpeas, rinsed and drained
- 1 small red onion, finely chopped
- 1 ripe avocado, mashed
- 2 Tbls fresh cilantro, chopped
- 1 Tbls curry powder
- Juice of 1 lime
- Salt and pepper to taste
- 4 large whole grain tortillas
- 1 C. baby spinach leaves

DIRECTIONS:
- Mash chickpeas in a mixing bowl until chunky
- Add onion, avocado, cilantro, curry powder, lime juice, salt, and pepper, mixing until well combined
- Lay tortillas flat and distribute spinach leaves on each
- Spoon chickpea mixture onto the center of each tortilla
- Fold sides of tortilla then roll up snugly

TIPS:
- For extra zing, add a splash of hot sauce or a tsp of grated ginger

- Tortillas can be gently warmed for easier rolling

N.V. : Calories: 340, Fat: 9g, Carbs: 55g, Protein: 12g, Sugar: 7g

ASIAN TOFU LETTUCE WRAPS

PREPARATION TIME: 20 min

COOKING TIME: 10 min

SERVINGS: 4

M.OF COOKING: Sautéing

INGREDIENTS:

- 14 oz. firm tofu, pressed and cubed
- 2 Tbls sesame oil
- 1 Tbls tamari or soy sauce
- 1 Tbls hoisin sauce
- 1 clove garlic, minced
- 1 tsp freshly grated ginger
- 1 C. julienned carrots
- 1 C. sliced red bell pepper
- 1 C. mung bean sprouts
- 8 large lettuce leaves (e.g., Butter or Bibb lettuce)

DIRECTIONS:

- Heat sesame oil in a skillet over medium-high heat
- Add tofu and cook until golden brown, stirring occasionally, about 7 min
- Add tamari, hoisin sauce, garlic, and ginger to tofu and stir to coat
- Cook for another 3 min
- Remove from heat and mix in carrots, bell pepper, and bean sprouts
- Divide filling among lettuce leaves, wrapping to enclose the filling

TIPS:

- Wraps can be served with a side of extra tamari for dipping
- For added crunch, top with chopped peanuts or cashews

N.V. : Calories: 210, Fat: 12g, Carbs: 16g, Protein: 14g, Sugar: 5g

GRILLED VEGGIE AND HUMMUS PITA

PREPARATION TIME: 25 min

COOKING TIME: 10 min

SERVINGS: 4

M.OF COOKING: Grilling

INGREDIENTS:

- 1 medium zucchini, sliced lengthwise
- 1 red bell pepper, seeded and quartered
- 1 yellow bell pepper, seeded and quartered
- 1 eggplant, sliced into ½-inch rounds
- 2 Tbls extra-virgin olive oil
- Salt and pepper to taste
- 4 whole grain pita breads
- 1 C. hummus
- 1 C. baby arugula

DIRECTIONS:

- Preheat grill to medium-high heat (375°F or 190°C)
- Brush zucchini, bell peppers, and eggplant with olive oil and season with salt and pepper
- Grill vegetables until tender and charred, about 4-5 min per side
- Spread hummus inside pita breads evenly
- Stuff pitas with grilled vegetables and arugula

TIPS:

- Grilled vegetables can be substituted with any seasonal veggies of your choice
- If hummus is too thick, thin it out with a little bit of olive oil for easier spreading

N.V. : Calories: 330, Fat: 14g, Carbs: 45g, Protein: 12g, Sugar: 8g

ROASTED BEET AND GOAT CHEESE BAGUETTE

PREPARATION TIME: 30 min

COOKING TIME: 20 min

SERVINGS: 4

M. OF COOKING: Roasting

INGREDIENTS:

- 4 small beets, peeled and thinly sliced
- 2 Tbls balsamic vinegar
- 1 Tbls extra-virgin olive oil
- Salt and fresh ground pepper to taste
- 1 baguette, sliced in half lengthwise
- 4 oz. goat cheese
- 1 C. baby spinach leaves
- ¼ C. walnuts, toasted and chopped

DIRECTIONS:

- Preheat oven to 400°F (200°C)
- Toss beets with balsamic vinegar, olive oil, salt, and pepper
- Roast on a lined baking sheet until tender and slightly caramelized, about 20 min
- Spread goat cheese on the halved baguette
- Layer roasted beets, spinach, and sprinkle walnuts over goat cheese
- Assemble sandwich by placing the two halves together

TIPS:

- For a more robust flavor, drizzle with a little honey over the beets before assembling the sandwich
- Walnuts can be replaced with pecans for a different texture

N.V. : Calories: 410, Fat: 18g, Carbs: 50g, Protein: 14g, Sugar: 9g

MEDITERRANEAN CHICKPEA PITA POCKETS

PREPARATION TIME: 15 min

COOKING TIME: none

SERVINGS: 4

M. OF COOKING: No Cooking

INGREDIENTS:

- 1 C. canned chickpeas, rinsed and drained
- 1 small cucumber, diced
- 1 C. cherry tomatoes, halved
- ½ C. red onion, thinly sliced
- ¼ C. kalamata olives, pitted and sliced
- 1 Tbls fresh dill, chopped
- Juice of 1 lemon
- 2 Tbls extra-virgin olive oil
- Salt and pepper to taste
- 4 whole wheat pita pockets
- ½ C. tzatziki sauce

DIRECTIONS:

- In a bowl, combine chickpeas, cucumber, cherry tomatoes, red onion, olives, dill, lemon juice, olive oil, salt, and pepper, tossing to mix well
- Cut a slit in each pita to form a pocket
- Spread tzatziki sauce inside the pita pockets
- Stuff the chickpea mixture into the pita pockets

TIPS:

- To enhance flavors, allow the chickpea mixture to marinate in the fridge for 30 min before stuffing the pita pockets
- Pitas can be lightly toasted before assembling for added warmth and texture

N.V. : Calories: 290, Fat: 9g, Carbs: 45g, Protein: 9g, Sugar: 6g

SPICY SHRIMP AVOCADO WRAP

PREPARATION TIME: 20 min

COOKING TIME: 5 min

SERVINGS: 4

M. OF COOKING: Sautéing

INGREDIENTS:

- 1 lb. shrimp, peeled and deveined
- 1 Tbls Cajun seasoning

- 1 Tbls coconut oil
- 2 ripe avocados, sliced
- 1 small red cabbage, shredded
- 1 small carrot, julienned
- 2 Tbls fresh cilantro, chopped
- 4 large whole grain tortillas
- 1 lime, cut into wedges

DIRECTIONS:

- Season shrimp with Cajun seasoning
- Heat coconut oil in a skillet over medium-high heat and sauté shrimp until pink and cooked through, about 3-4 min
- Warm tortillas in a dry skillet
- Divide avocado slices, shredded cabbage, and julienned carrot equally among tortillas
- Add cooked shrimp and sprinkle with cilantro
- Squeeze lime over the filling
- Fold and roll tortillas to close

TIPS:

- Personalize the spice level by adjusting the amount of Cajun seasoning to taste
- Serve with additional lime wedges for extra brightness

N.V. : Calories: 360, Fat: 16g, Carbs: 28g, Protein: 25g, Sugar: 5g

SUNDRIED TOMATO BASIL TURKEY WRAP

PREPARATION TIME: 10 min
COOKING TIME: none

SERVINGS: 4
M. OF COOKING: No Cooking
INGREDIENTS:

- 8 oz. sliced turkey breast
- 1 C. baby spinach
- ½ C. sundried tomatoes, drained and chopped
- ¼ C. fresh basil leaves, chopped
- 2 Tbls extra-virgin olive oil
- 1 Tbls balsamic vinegar
- 4 large spinach wraps
- 1 C. shredded mozzarella cheese

DIRECTIONS:

- In a bowl, toss sundried tomatoes with basil, olive oil, and balsamic vinegar
- Spread the mixture onto the spinach wraps
- Layer sliced turkey breast on top of the tomato mixture
- Add spinach leaves and mozzarella cheese
- Roll the wraps tightly, tucking in sides

TIPS:

- Experiment with different types of cheese such as feta or goat cheese for a different flavor profile
- Wraps can be gently toasted on a dry skillet for a crunchy texture

N.V. : Calories: 320, Fat: 16g, Carbs: 28g, Protein: 20g, Sugar: 6g

Chapter 4: Satisfying Dinner Delights

4.1 Plant-Based Power Plates

As the sun dips below the horizon, signaling the close of our bustling days, our hearts and kitchens come alive with the promise of dinner—a time to replenish and savor. In this lovingly curated section, we'll explore the rich tapestry of plant-based power plates that marry nutrition with satiating flavors. Imagine dishes that are a canvas of vibrant vegetables, whole grains, and legumes, each a brushstroke of Mother Nature's pure palette. But these meals aren't just feasts for the eyes; they're bastions of energy, lovingly designed to fuel your body and delight your soul. From the subtle, earthy notes of a mushroom lentil loaf to the zestful zing in a quinoa and black bean salad, every recipe is a stepping stone towards a more vibrant you. Let these dishes be your gentle, empowering guide to a table brimming with the joys of healthful, plant-based eating. With each bite, we affirm our commitment to a lifestyle of wholesomeness, one delectable dinner at a time.

Socca Pizza with Sun-Dried Tomato Pesto

Preparation Time: 15 min
Cooking Time: 20 min
Servings: 4
M. of Cooking: Oven Baking
Ingredients:
- 1 C. chickpea flour
- 1 ¼ C. water
- ¼ C. extra virgin olive oil
- Salt to taste
- ½ C. sun-dried tomatoes, oil-packed and drained
- 1 C. fresh basil leaves
- 1 garlic clove
- 2 Tbls pine nuts
- ½ C. arugula
- ¼ C. olives, pitted and sliced
- ¼ red onion, thinly sliced

Directions:
- Whisk together chickpea flour, water, 1 Tbls olive oil, and salt, let batter rest for 30 min
- Preheat oven to 450°F (232°C)
- Pour batter onto greased baking sheet, bake until edges are crispy, about 10 min
- For pesto, blend sun-dried tomatoes, basil, garlic, pine nuts, and remaining olive oil until smooth

- Spread pesto on the baked socca crust, top with arugila, olives, and onion, bake for an additional 10 min

TIPS:

- Substitute arugula with spinach for a milder flavor

- Add chili flakes to the pesto for an extra kick

- Sprinkle nutritional yeast on top before serving for a cheesy flavor

N.V. : Calories: 290, Fat: 17g, Carbs: 27g, Protein: 8g, Sugar: 4g

GRILLED PORTOBELLO STEAKS WITH AVOCADO CHIMICHURRI

PREPARATION TIME: 10 min

COOKING TIME: 8 min

SERVINGS: 4

M.OF COOKING: Grilling

INGREDIENTS:

- 4 large portobello mushrooms
- 2 Tbls balsamic vinegar
- 1 Tbls soy sauce
- 1 Tbls olive oil
- 1 ripe avocado
- 1 C. fresh parsley
- ¼ C. cilantro
- 3 Tbls red wine vinegar
- 1 garlic clove
- 1 tsp red chili flakes
- ½ tsp cumin
- Salt and pepper to taste

DIRECTIONS:

- Remove portobello stems and gills, marinate caps in balsamic vinegar, soy sauce, and olive oil for 10 min

- Grill over medium heat for 4 min per side

- For the chimichurri, pulse avocado, parsley, cilantro, red wine vinegar, garlic,

chili flakes, cumin, salt, and pepper until smooth

- Serve mushrooms topped with the avocado chimichurri

TIPS:

- Use the portobello stems in a stir-fry to minimize waste

- Prepare the chimichurri ahead of time and refrigerate to let flavors meld

- Serve with quinoa for a complete protein meal

N.V. : Calories: 210, Fat: 14g, Carbs: 19g, Protein: 5g, Sugar: 5g

ROASTED RAINBOW BOWL WITH TAHINI DRIZZLE

PREPARATION TIME: 20 min

COOKING TIME: 25 min

SERVINGS: 4

M.OF COOKING: Roasting

INGREDIENTS:

- 1 small butternut squash, peeled and cubed
- 1 beet, peeled and cubed
- 1 Tbls coconut oil, melted
- Salt and black pepper to taste
- 2 C. kale, chopped
- 1 Tbls lemon juice
- 1 C. quinoa, cooked
- 1 C. chickpeas, rinsed and drained
- ¼ C. tahini
- 1 garlic clove, minced
- ¼ C. warm water
- 1 tsp maple syrup

DIRECTIONS:

- Toss butternut squash and beet with coconut oil, salt, and pepper, roast at 425°F (218°C) for 25 min

- Massage kale with lemon juice until tender

- Arrange quinoa, roasted veggies, chickpeas, and kale in bowls
- Whisk tahini, garlic, warm water, and maple syrup, drizzle over bowls

TIPS:

- Massage the kale with a bit of olive oil as well for added richness
- Roast some sunflower seeds alongside the veggies for a crunchy garnish
- Add a pinch of cinnamon to roasted squash for a subtle spiced flavor

N.V. : Calories: 400, Fat: 14g, Carbs: 58g, Protein: 13g, Sugar: 7g

SPICED LENTIL STUFFED ACORN SQUASH

PREPARATION TIME: 15 min

COOKING TIME: 1 hr

SERVINGS: 4

M.OF COOKING: Baking

INGREDIENTS:

- 2 acorn squashes, halved and seeded
- 1 C. green lentils
- 1 Tbls grapeseed oil
- 1 small onion, diced
- 2 garlic cloves, minced
- 1 tsp ground coriander
- 1 tsp ground cumin
- ½ tsp ground cinnamon
- ¼ C. dried cranberries
- 2 Tbls pumpkin seeds
- Fresh cilantro, chopped, for garnish
- Salt and pepper to taste

DIRECTIONS:

- Preheat oven to 375°F (190°C)
- Bake squash halves cut-side down until tender, about 40 min
- Cook lentils according to package instructions
- Sauté onion and garlic in grapeseed oil, add spices and cooked lentils, cook for 5 min

- Stir in cranberries and pumpkin seeds, stuff into squash halves, bake for an additional 20 min
- Garnish with cilantro before serving

TIPS:

- The lentil stuffing can be prepared in advance and stored in the fridge
- Serve with a dollop of Greek yogurt to balance the flavors
- Swap cranberries for pomegranate seeds for a juicier bite

N.V. : Calories: 365, Fat: 7g, Carbs: 65g, Protein: 14g, Sugar: 5g

CAULIFLOWER STEAKS WITH ROMESCO SAUCE

PREPARATION TIME: 10 min

COOKING TIME: 30 min

SERVINGS: 4

M.OF COOKING: Roasting

INGREDIENTS:

- 1 large head cauliflower, cut into steaks
- 2 Tbls avocado oil
- Salt and pepper to taste
- 1 red bell pepper, roasted and peeled
- ½ C. almonds, toasted
- 1 garlic clove
- 1 Tbls tomato paste
- 1 tsp smoked paprika
- 2 Tbls red wine vinegar
- 1 Tbls extra virgin olive oil
- Fresh parsley, for garnish

DIRECTIONS:

- Preheat oven to 400°F (204°C)
- Brush cauliflower steaks with avocado oil, season with salt and pepper, roast until golden, about 25-30 min
- Blend bell pepper, almonds, garlic, tomato paste, smoked paprika, vinegar, and olive oil until smooth

- Serve cauliflower steaks with romesco sauce, garnish with parsley

TIPS:

- Romesco sauce can be used as a dip or spread for other dishes
- For a nut-free version, use sunflower seeds instead of almonds
- Garnish with chopped roasted red peppers for added texture

N.V. : Calories: 220, Fat: 18g, Carbs: 14g, Protein: 6g, Sugar: 5g

ZUCCHINI NOODLE PAD THAI

PREPARATION TIME: 20 min

COOKING TIME: 10 min

SERVINGS: 4

M.OF COOKING: Sautéing

INGREDIENTS:

- 4 zucchinis, spiralized
- 1 Tbls sesame oil
- 1 red bell pepper, thinly sliced
- 1 carrot, julienned
- 1 C. purple cabbage, shredded
- ½ C. edamame, shelled
- 1 Tbls ginger, minced
- 2 garlic cloves, minced
- 2 Tbls almond butter
- 1 Tbls tamarind paste
- 1 Tbls maple syrup
- 2 Tbls lime juice
- 1 Tbls coconut aminos
- Crushed peanuts and green onions for garnish

DIRECTIONS:

- Sauté red bell pepper, carrot, cabbage, and edamame in sesame oil until just tender
- Add ginger and garlic, cook for 1 min
- Whisk together almond butter, tamarind paste, maple syrup, lime juice, and coconut aminos

- Toss zucchini noodles and sauce in pan, heat through
- Garnish with peanuts and green onions

TIPS:

- Do not overcook the zucchini noodles to retain a crunchy texture
- For added protein, toss in fried tofu cubes
- Squeeze extra lime juice on top right before serving for a tangy kick

N.V. : Calories: 190, Fat: 8g, Carbs: 24g, Protein: 7g, Sugar: 12g

MOROCCAN SPICED CHICKPEA BOWL

PREPARATION TIME: 15 min

COOKING TIME: 30 min

SERVINGS: 4

M.OF COOKING: Simmering

INGREDIENTS:

- 2 C. chickpeas, rinsed and drained
- 1 Tbls olive oil
- 1 onion, chopped
- 3 garlic cloves, minced
- 1 tsp ground cumin
- 1 tsp ground coriander
- ½ tsp ground cinnamon
- ½ tsp ground turmeric
- ¼ tsp cayenne pepper
- 1 C. diced tomatoes
- 4 C. spinach
- 1 C. couscous, cooked
- Lemon wedges and fresh mint for serving

DIRECTIONS:

- Heat olive oil, sate onion, and garlic until translucent
- Stir in cumin, coriander, cinnamon, turmeric, and cayenne, cook for 1 min
- Add chickpeas and tomatoes, simmer for 25 min
- Stir in spinach until wilted, remove from heat

- Serve chickpea mixture over couscous with lemon wedges and mint

TIPS:
- Serve with a dollop of harissa for extra heat
- Garnish with pomegranate seeds for a sweet contrast

- Replace couscous with cauliflower rice for a lower-carb option

N.V. : Calories: 330, Fat: 6g, Carbs: 56g, Protein: 13g, Sugar: 8g

4.2 LEAN MEAT AND SEAFOOD ENTREES

Welcome to the heart of homely warmth and well-being—the dinner table. As dusk settles and the home buzzes with the day's end, it's time to gather and nourish both body and spirit. In this section, we'll explore the delectable world of lean meats and seafood, infusing your meals with flavors that delight without sacrificing nutrition.

Lean proteins are like the quiet champions of a whole food diet—unassuming yet powerful in their ability to fuel our bodies with essential nutrients. Whether it's the tender pull of perfectly cooked chicken, the robust heartiness of a succulent steak, or the delicate flakiness of a seared fish fillet, each dish offers a symphony of taste and wholesomeness.

Embrace the ocean's bounty and the land's finest cuts as we journey through thoughtfully curated entrees designed to appease the palate and build a fortress of health. Prepare to be enchanted by recipes that promise satisfaction without complexity, bringing joy to your table with each and every bite.

CITRUS-HERB GRILLED TROUT

PREPARATION TIME: 15 min.

COOKING TIME: 10 min.

SERVINGS: 4

M.OF COOKING: Grilling

INGREDIENTS:
- 4 whole trout, cleaned and scales removed
- 1 lemon, thinly sliced
- 2 sprigs fresh thyme
- 2 sprigs fresh rosemary
- 2 cloves garlic, minced
- 1 Tbls extra-virgin olive oil
- Sea salt to taste
- Freshly ground black pepper to taste

DIRECTIONS:
- Preheat grill to medium-high heat, about 400°F (204°C)
- Rub the inside of each trout with garlic, and drizzle with olive oil
- Season with salt and pepper
- Stuff the cavity with lemon slices, thyme, and rosemary
- Grill trout for 5 min. on each side or until the fish flakes easily with a fork

TIPS:
- Serve with a side of grilled vegetables for a complete meal

- Use a fish basket for easy flipping on the grill

N.V. : Calories: 297, Fat: 13g, Carbs: 1g, Protein: 42g, Sugar: 0g

SPICED LAMB KOFTAS WITH TZATZIKI

PREPARATION TIME: 25 min.

COOKING TIME: 15 min.

SERVINGS: 6

M.OF COOKING: Grilling

INGREDIENTS:

- 1 lb. ground lamb
- 1 medium onion, finely chopped
- 2 cloves garlic, minced
- 1 Tbls garam masala
- 1 tsp cumin
- 1 tsp paprika
- ½ tsp cinnamon
- ½ tsp cayenne pepper
- Salt to taste
- Freshly ground black pepper to taste
- Mint leaves for garnish
- Non-fat Greek yogurt for tzatziki
- 1 cucumber, grated for tzatziki
- 2 cloves garlic, minced for tzatziki
- 1 Tbls fresh dill, chopped for tzatziki

DIRECTIONS:

- Combine ground lamb, onion, garlic, garam masala, cumin, paprika, cinnamon, cayenne, salt, and black pepper in a bowl and mix well
- Shape mixture into oval-shaped patties and grill over medium heat for about 7-8 min. on each side or until cooked through
- Mix Greek yogurt, cucumber, garlic, and dill for tzatziki and chill

TIPS:

- Serve with tzatziki and a sprinkle of mint leaves

- Can be served inside pita bread with fresh veggies

N.V. : Calories: 256, Fat: 17g, Carbs: 5g, Protein: 19g, Sugar: 3g

CHIMICHURRI FLANK STEAK

PREPARATION TIME: 1 hr. 20 min.

COOKING TIME: 15 min.

SERVINGS: 6

M.OF COOKING: Grilling

INGREDIENTS:

- 2 lb. flank steak
- Marinade: ½ C. fresh parsley, chopped
- ¼ C. fresh cilantro, chopped
- 3 Tbls red wine vinegar
- 4 cloves garlic, minced
- 1 tsp dried oregano
- ½ tsp crushed red pepper flakes
- ½ C. extra-virgin olive oil
- Salt to taste
- Freshly ground black pepper to taste

DIRECTIONS:

- Mix parsley, cilantro, vinegar, garlic, oregano, and red pepper flakes in a bowl and slowly whisk in olive oil
- Season the flank steak with salt and pepper and coat with the chimichurri sauce
- Marinate for at least 1 hr
- Preheat grill to high heat, around 450°F (232°C) and grill the steak for 7 min. on one side, then turn and grill for another 7 min.

TIPS:

- Let the steak rest for 10 min. before slicing against the grain
- Reserve some marinade to serve as a sauce

N.V. : Calories: 410, Fat: 30g, Carbs: 2g, Protein: 32g, Sugar: 0g

PISTACHIO-CRUSTED SALMON

PREPARATION TIME: 10 min.

COOKING TIME: 12 min.

SERVINGS: 4

M.OF COOKING: Baking

INGREDIENTS:

- 4 salmon fillets, 6 oz. each
- ½ C. shelled pistachios, finely chopped
- 1 Tbls Dijon mustard
- 1 Tbls honey
- 1 Tbls extra-virgin olive oil
- Zest of 1 lemon
- Salt to taste
- Freshly ground black pepper to taste

DIRECTIONS:

- Preheat oven to 375°F (190°C)
- Mix pistachios, Dijon mustard, honey, olive oil, and lemon zest in a bowl
- Season salmon with salt and pepper
- Press the pistachio mixture on top of each salmon fillet
- Place fillets on a baking sheet and bake for 12 min. or until salmon is opaque

TIPS:

- Use a food processor to get evenly chopped pistachios
- The crust should be golden and crunchy

N.V. : Calories: 345, Fat: 19g, Carbs: 9g, Protein: 34g, Sugar: 5g

THAI BASIL CHICKEN STIR-FRY

PREPARATION TIME: 25 min.

COOKING TIME: 10 min.

SERVINGS: 4

M.OF COOKING: Stir-Frying

INGREDIENTS:

- 1 lb. chicken breast, thinly sliced
- 2 Tbls avocado oil
- 3 cloves garlic, minced
- 1 red bell pepper, sliced
- 1 yellow bell pepper, sliced
- 1 onion, sliced
- 1 C. Thai basil leaves
- Sauce: 2 Tbls fish sauce
- 1 Tbls soy sauce
- 1 Tbls oyster sauce
- 1 tsp coconut sugar
- ½ tsp white pepper

DIRECTIONS:

- Heat oil in a wok over high heat
- Sauté garlic until fragrant
- Add chicken and stir-fry until browned
- Add bell peppers and onion and cook until just tender
- Mix fish sauce, soy sauce, oyster sauce, coconut sugar, and pepper in a bowl
- Pour the sauce over the chicken mixture and stir-fry for 2 more min.
- Remove from heat and stir in Thai basil leaves

TIPS:

- Serve with steamed brown rice for a complete meal
- Add a dash of chili flakes for extra heat

N.V. : Calories: 282, Fat: 9g, Carbs: 11g, Protein: 39g, Sugar: 6g

SEARED SCALLOPS WITH CAULIFLOWER PURÉE

PREPARATION TIME: 20 min.

COOKING TIME: 15 min.

SERVINGS: 4

M.OF COOKING: Sautéing

INGREDIENTS:

- 12 large sea scallops
- 1 Tbls ghee
- Salt to taste
- Freshly ground black pepper to taste
- 1 head cauliflower, cut into florets

- 2 Tbls unsalted butter
- ¼ C. unsweetened almond milk
- 1 Tbls fresh chives, chopped for garnish

DIRECTIONS:

- Steam cauliflower until very tender
- Blend steamed cauliflower, butter, and almond milk in a food processor until smooth to make the purée
- Pat scallops dry and season with salt and pepper
- Heat ghee in a pan over high heat and sear scallops for about 2 min. on each side or until a golden crust forms

TIPS:

- Avoid overcrowding the pan when searing scallops
- Drizzle purée with truffle oil for added flavor

N.V. : Calories: 234, Fat: 12g, Carbs: 13g, Protein: 19g, Sugar: 5g

PEPPER-CRUSTED BEEF TENDERLOIN WITH HORSERADISH CREAM

PREPARATION TIME: 30 min.

COOKING TIME: 1 hr.

SERVINGS: 8

M.OF COOKING: Roasting

INGREDIENTS:

- 3 lb. beef tenderloin
- 2 Tbls whole black peppercorns, crushed
- 2 Tbls sea salt
- 2 Tbls avocado oil
- Horseradish cream: 1 C. sour cream
- ¼ C. prepared horseradish
- 1 Tbls Dijon mustard
- 1 tsp apple cider vinegar
- Salt to taste
- Chopped fresh chives for garnish

DIRECTIONS:

- Preheat oven to 425°F (218°C)
- Rub the tenderloin with crushed peppercorns, salt, and oil
- Roast in the oven for 45-55 min. or until desired doneness
- Mix sour cream, horseradish, mustard, vinegar, and salt to make the horseradish cream
- Let the beef rest for 10 min. before slicing

TIPS:

- Serve with horseradish cream on the side
- Pair with roasted root vegetables for a hearty meal

N.V. : Calories: 498, Fat: 31g, Carbs: 3g, Protein: 50g, Sugar: 2g

As the sun dips below the horizon and the comforting embrace of evening unfolds, dinner calls us to gather and nourish both body and soul. Within this sacred time, our focus turns to crafting sides that do more than just satisfy; they soothe, they enrich, and they complete our plate with a warm, wholesome touch. Here, we celebrate the unsung heroes of our dinner table—the vibrant, nutrient-dense whole grains and vegetables that stand ready to transform your mealtime into a symphony of flavors and textures.

In this section, we'll delve into the art of combining fibrous, earthy grains with the natural sweetness and robustness of garden vegetables. Marrying these elements is not just an act of culinary balance but an opportunity to provide comfort in every forkful. From the nutty allure of quinoa paired with the delicate charms of roasted Brussels sprouts to the heartiness of farro adorned with the sunset hues of butternut squash, each recipe is an invitation: to slow down, to savor, and to feed your joy with the simple pleasures of food made with reverence for its sources. Let these sides be your canvas for creativity and your vessel for vitality as we cherish the natural abundance that graces our plates.

QUINOA TABBOULEH WITH CHARRED CORN

PREPARATION TIME: 20 min

COOKING TIME: 15 min

SERVINGS: 6

M. OF COOKING: Stovetop

INGREDIENTS:

- 1 C. quinoa, rinsed
- 2 C. water
- 2 ears of corn, husks removed
- 1 large cucumber, diced
- 1 pint cherry tomatoes, halved
- 1 red onion, finely chopped
- ¾ C. fresh parsley, chopped
- ¼ C. fresh mint, chopped
- ⅓ C. extra virgin olive oil
- 3 Tbls lemon juice
- Salt and black pepper to taste

DIRECTIONS:

- Combine quinoa and water in a pot and bring to a boil, reduce heat to low, cover, and simmer until quinoa is tender and water is absorbed, about 15 min
- While quinoa cooks, grill corn over medium heat, turning frequently until kernels are slightly charred, let cool, then slice kernels from cob
- In a large bowl, combine cooked quinoa, charred corn, cucumber, cherry tomatoes, red onion, parsley, and mint
- Drizzle with olive oil and lemon juice, season with salt and pepper, and toss gently to combine

TIPS:

- To enhance the smoky flavor, add a pinch of smoked paprika to the salad
- Quinoa can be cooked in a rice cooker for added convenience
- This dish can be served warm or chilled, making it perfect for meal prep

N.V. : Calories: 258, Fat: 10g, Carbs: 36g, Protein: 6g, Sugar: 5g

MILLET PILAF WITH ROASTED ROOT VEGETABLES

PREPARATION TIME: 15 min

COOKING TIME: 40 min

SERVINGS: 4

M.OF COOKING: Oven, Stovetop

INGREDIENTS:

- 1 C. millet
- 2 C. vegetable broth
- 1 lb. mixed root vegetables (beets, carrots, parsnips), peeled and diced
- 1 Tbls coconut oil, melted
- 1 tsp fresh thyme leaves
- Salt and black pepper to taste
- 2 Tbls pumpkin seeds, toasted
- 1 Tbls apple cider vinegar

DIRECTIONS:

- Preheat oven to 400°F (200°C)
- Toss root vegetables with coconut oil, thyme, salt, and pepper, spread evenly on a baking sheet, and roast until tender, about 30 min
- Toast millet in a dry saucepan over medium heat until fragrant, about 2 min
- Add vegetable broth, bring to a boil, reduce heat to low, cover, and simmer until millet is tender and broth is absorbed, about 20 min
- Fluff millet with a fork, then fold in roasted vegetables, top with toasted pumpkin seeds, and drizzle with apple cider vinegar before serving

TIPS:

- Roast the root vegetables ahead of time to cut down on day-of prep time
- Refrigerate leftovers to create a delightful cold millet salad the next day

- Use other nuts or seeds like almonds or sunflower seeds for an alternative crunch

N.V. : Calories: 305, Fat: 9g, Carbs: 50g, Protein: 8g, Sugar: 7g

BUCKWHEAT WITH CARAMELIZED SHALLOTS AND SWISS CHARD

PREPARATION TIME: 10 min

COOKING TIME: 25 min

SERVINGS: 4

M.OF COOKING: Stovetop

INGREDIENTS:

- 1 C. buckwheat groats
- 2 C. water
- 3 Tbls olive oil
- 6 shallots, thinly sliced
- 1 bunch Swiss chard, stems removed, leaves chopped
- Salt and black pepper to taste
- 2 tsp balsamic vinegar
- ⅓ C. walnuts, chopped and toasted

DIRECTIONS:

- Combine buckwheat groats and water in a pot, bring to a boil, then reduce heat to low, cover, and cook until tender and water is absorbed, about 20 min
- Heat olive oil in a pan over medium heat, add shallots, and cook, stirring occasionally, until they are golden and caramelized, about 15 min
- Add Swiss chard to pan, season with salt and pepper, cook until wilted
- Stir in balsamic vinegar
- Mix caramelized shallot and Swiss chard mixture with cooked buckwheat, sprinkle with toasted walnuts before serving

TIPS:

- Caramelizing the shallots slowly on low heat brings out their natural sweetness

- Buckwheat can be replaced with kasha for a toasted flavor variation
- Serve alongside a protein of choice for a complete meal

N.V. : Calories: 280, Fat: 9g, Carbs: 44g, Protein: 8g, Sugar: 5g

FARRO WITH GRILLED ASPARAGUS AND LEMON ZEST

PREPARATION TIME: 10 min
COOKING TIME: 30 min
SERVINGS: 6
M.OF COOKING: Grill, Stovetop
INGREDIENTS:

- 1½ C. farro, rinsed
- 3 C. water
- 1 lb. asparagus, trimmed
- 2 Tbls olive oil
- 1 lemon, zest and juice
- Salt and black pepper to taste
- ¼ C. Parmesan cheese, freshly grated
- ¼ C. fresh basil leaves, thinly sliced

DIRECTIONS:

- Soak farro in water for 10 min, then drain and rinse
- Bring 3 C. of water to a boil in a pot, add farro, reduce heat to low, cover, and simmer until al dente, about 20 min
- Preheat grill to medium-high, toss asparagus with 1 Tbls olive oil, season with salt and pepper, grill until tender and slightly charred, about 10 min, then chop into 2-inch pieces
- In a large bowl, combine cooked farro, grilled asparagus, lemon zest and juice, remaining olive oil, tossing to combine
- Season to taste with salt and pepper, sprinkle with Parmesan and fresh basil

TIPS:

- Soaking the farro shortens cooking time and makes it more digestible
- Use a vegetable peeler to create thin Parmesan shavings for garnish
- This side pairs excellently with grilled fish or chicken

N.V. : Calories: 260, Fat: 7g, Carbs: 42g, Protein: 9g, Sugar: 2g

TOASTED QUINOA WITH ROASTED BUTTERNUT SQUASH

PREPARATION TIME: 15 min
COOKING TIME: 30 min
SERVINGS: 4
M.OF COOKING: Roasting
INGREDIENTS:

- 1 C. quinoa, rinsed
- 2 C. vegetable broth
- 1 medium butternut squash, peeled and diced
- 1 Tbls olive oil
- 1 tsp smoked paprika
- 1/2 tsp ground cumin
- Salt and pepper to taste
- 1/4 C. dried cranberries
- 1/4 C. pumpkin seeds, toasted

DIRECTIONS:

- Preheat oven to 425°F (220°C)
- Toss butternut squash in olive oil, smoked paprika, cumin, salt, and pepper and spread on a baking sheet
- Roast until tender and slightly caramelized, about 25-30 min
- Meanwhile, bring quinoa and vegetable broth to a boil in a saucepan
- Reduce heat, cover, and simmer until quinoa is fluffy and liquid is absorbed, about 15 min

- Combine roasted squash with quinoa, then stir in cranberries and pumpkin seeds before serving

TIPS:

- To enhance the nuttiness of quinoa, toast it in a dry skillet before boiling
- Incorporate a handful of fresh arugula for a peppery punch
- Drizzle with balsamic reduction for added depth of flavor

N.V. : Calories: 315, Fat: 7g, Carbs: 55g, Protein: 8g, Sugar: 7g

MILLET PILAF WITH CARAMELIZED ONIONS AND MUSHROOMS

PREPARATION TIME: 10 min

COOKING TIME: 25 min

SERVINGS: 6

M.OF COOKING: Simmering

INGREDIENTS:

- 1 C. millet
- 2 C. low-sodium chicken broth
- 1 Tbls extra virgin olive oil
- 2 large onions, thinly sliced
- 8 oz. cremini mushrooms, sliced
- 2 cloves garlic, minced
- 1/4 tsp thyme, dried
- Salt and pepper to taste
- Fresh parsley, chopped for garnish

DIRECTIONS:

- Toast millet in a dry pan until golden brown, stirring frequently, about 3 min
- Add chicken broth, bring to a boil, then reduce heat to low, cover, and simmer for 20 min
- In a separate pan, heat olive oil over medium-high heat
- Add onions and cook until they start to caramelize, about 10 min

- Add mushrooms, garlic, and thyme, and cook until mushrooms are soft and browned, about 8 min
- Combine millet with caramelized onions and mushrooms, season with salt and pepper to taste
- Garnish with fresh parsley before serving

TIPS:

- Try adding a splash of white wine to the mushrooms as they cook for additional flavor
- If millet is unavailable, whole grain bulgur or farro make great substitutes
- Millet can be cooked in advance to cut down on preparation time

N.V. : Calories: 240, Fat: 5g, Carbs: 42g, Protein: 6g, Sugar: 2g

BARLEY AND POMEGRANATE TABBOULEH

PREPARATION TIME: 20 min

COOKING TIME: 40 min

SERVINGS: 6

M.OF COOKING: Boiling

INGREDIENTS:

- 1 C. hulled barley
- 3 C. water
- 1 large cucumber, seeded and diced
- 1/2 C. pomegranate seeds
- 1/4 C. mint leaves, finely chopped
- 1/4 C. flat-leaf parsley, finely chopped
- 3 Tbls olive oil
- Juice of 1 lemon
- Salt and pepper to taste
- 1/4 tsp allspice

DIRECTIONS:

- Rinse barley under cold water and drain
- In a medium saucepan, combine the barley with water, bring to a boil, then reduce heat, cover, and simmer until barley is tender and water is absorbed, about 40 min
- Let cool to room temp.

- In a large bowl, combine cooked barley, cucumber, pomegranate seeds, mint, and parsley
- In a small bowl, whisk together olive oil, lemon juice, salt, pepper, and allspice
- Pour dressing over barley mixture and toss to coat evenly

TIPS:

- To release more juice from the lemon, roll it on the countertop before cutting and squeezing
- For extra crunch, add a handful of chopped walnuts
- Can be served chilled or at room temperature for varying textures

N.V. : Calories: 202, Fat: 7g, Carbs: 34g, Protein: 4g, Sugar: 3g

CHAPTER 5: SNACKS AND SIDES

5.1 QUICK AND EASY VEGETABLE SNACKS

In our bustling world, it's easy to succumb to the siren call of processed snacks, but the heart of wholesome snacking lies in the earth's own offerings—vegetables. "Quick and Easy Vegetable Snacks" is your invitation to rediscover the crunch and color of nature's bounty in bites that are as nourishing as they are delightful. Here, I'll share with you a curation of snackable treasures that not only appease hunger pangs but infuse your body with the vitality it craves. You'll learn to transform humble veggies into vibrant snacks with a mere dappling of spices, a splash of creative dressing, or a simple roast to perfection. They are the perfect antidote for those mid-day lulls, post-workout replenishments, or the little hands seeking a munch. Turn the page, and let's embrace the art of snacking that is as kind to your body as it is to your schedule.

ZUCCHINI AND CARROT FRITTERS

PREPARATION TIME: 15 min.
COOKING TIME: 6 min.
SERVINGS: 8
M. OF COOKING: Pan Frying
INGREDIENTS:
- 2 medium zucchinis, grated
- 2 medium carrots, grated
- 2 green onions, finely chopped
- ¼ C. fresh parsley, minced
- ½ C. almond flour
- 1 large egg, beaten
- 2 Tbls coconut aminos
- 1 clove garlic, minced
- Virgin coconut oil for frying
- Sea salt to taste
- Freshly ground black pepper to taste

DIRECTIONS:
- Combine grated zucchini and carrots in a colander, sprinkle with a pinch of sea salt, and let sit to drain for 10 minutes
- Squeeze out excess moisture from the vegetables with a clean kitchen towel
- In a large bowl, mix together drained zucchini, carrots, green onions, parsley, almond flour, beaten egg, coconut aminos, minced garlic, sea salt, and black pepper until well combined
- Heat coconut oil in a skillet over medium heat
- Scoop spoonfuls of the zucchini and carrot mixture into the skillet and flatten to form fritters
- Fry until golden brown on each side, about 3 minutes per side

TIPS:

- Serve with a dollop of unsweetened Greek yogurt and a sprinkling of fresh herbs for added flavor
- For a crunchier exterior, fry in additional coconut oil
- Leftover fritters can be reheated in the oven to retain crispiness

N.V. : Calories: 88, Fat: 6g, Carbs: 7g, Protein: 4g, Sugar: 3g

CRISPY KALE CHIPS WITH TAHINI DRIZZLE

PREPARATION TIME: 10 min.

COOKING TIME: 15 min.

SERVINGS: 4

M.OF COOKING: Baking

INGREDIENTS:

- 1 bunch of kale, stems removed and leaves torn into bite-sized pieces
- 2 Tbls extra virgin olive oil
- 1 Tbls tahini
- 1 tsp smoked paprika
- ½ tsp garlic powder
- Sea salt to taste
- Freshly ground black pepper to taste

DIRECTIONS:

- Preheat oven to 350°F (175°C)
- In a large bowl, massage kale with olive oil until all pieces are lightly coated
- Sprinkle smoked paprika, garlic powder, sea salt, and black pepper over kale and toss to evenly distribute
- Spread kale in a single layer on a baking sheet lined with parchment paper
- Bake until edges are crispy but not burnt, about 15 minutes
- Drizzle tahini over baked kale chips before serving

TIPS:

- Let chips cool completely before drizzling to keep them crispy
- Use lacinato kale for a denser texture
- Add a squeeze of lemon juice to the tahini for a zesty twist

N.V. : Calories: 110, Fat: 9g, Carbs: 7g, Protein: 3g, Sugar: 0g

SPICY ROASTED CHICKPEAS

PREPARATION TIME: 5 min.

COOKING TIME: 40 min.

SERVINGS: 4

M.OF COOKING: Roasting

INGREDIENTS:

- 1 can (15 oz.) chickpeas, drained and rinsed
- 1 Tbls grapeseed oil
- 1 tsp chili powder
- ½ tsp ground cumin
- ¼ tsp cayenne pepper
- ¼ tsp sea salt

DIRECTIONS:

- Preheat oven to 400°F (200°C)
- Pat chickpeas dry with a clean kitchen towel
- In a bowl, toss chickpeas with grapeseed oil, chili powder, ground cumin, cayenne pepper, and sea salt until chickpeas are evenly coated
- Spread chickpeas on a baking sheet in a single layer
- Roast in the oven until crunchy, about 40 minutes, shaking the pan occasionally for even cooking

TIPS:

- Store leftover chickpeas in an airtight container to maintain crunchiness
- For extra heat, sprinkle additional cayenne pepper after roasting

- Can also be enjoyed as a crunchy salad topping

N.V. : Calories: 120, Fat: 4g, Carbs: 17g, Protein: 5g, Sugar: 0g

AVOCADO AND TOMATO STUFFED CUCUMBER BOATS

PREPARATION TIME: 20 min.

COOKING TIME: none

SERVINGS: 6

M. OF COOKING: No Cooking

INGREDIENTS:

- 3 medium cucumbers, halved lengthwise and seeds removed
- 1 ripe avocado, pitted and diced
- 1 pint cherry tomatoes, halved
- Juice of 1 lime
- 1 Tbls extra virgin olive oil
- 2 Tbls cilantro, chopped
- 1 small red onion, finely diced
- 1 jalapeño, seeds removed and minced
- Sea salt to taste
- Freshly ground black pepper to taste

DIRECTIONS:

- In a bowl, gently toss diced avocado, cherry tomatoes, lime juice, olive oil, cilantro, red onion, jalapeño, sea salt, and black pepper until combined
- Spoon the avocado and tomato mixture into the hollowed-out cucumbers
- Chill in the refrigerator until ready to serve

TIPS:

- Add a sprinkle of crumbled cotija cheese on top for a salty finish
- These cucumber boats can be made ahead and stored in an airtight container in the refrigerator
- For a protein boost, mix in shredded chicken or black beans

N.V. : Calories: 80, Fat: 6g, Carbs: 6g, Protein: 2g, Sugar: 3g

CRISPY KALE CHIPS WITH NUTRITIONAL YEAST

PREPARATION TIME: 10 min

COOKING TIME: 15 min

SERVINGS: 4

M. OF COOKING: Baking

INGREDIENTS:

- 1 bunch kale, tough stems removed
- 1 Tbls extra-virgin olive oil
- 2 Tbls nutritional yeast
- 1 tsp garlic powder
- ½ tsp smoked paprika
- ¼ tsp sea salt

DIRECTIONS:

- Preheat oven to 350°F (175°C)
- Tear kale leaves into bite-sized pieces
- In a bowl, drizzle kale with olive oil and toss until lightly coated
- Add nutritional yeast, garlic powder, smoked paprika, and sea salt; toss to distribute evenly
- Lay kale pieces on a baking sheet, ensuring they do not overlap
- Bake until edges are crispy but not burnt, about 15 min, rotating the sheet halfway through

TIPS:

- Massage the kale leaves with oil to make them extra crispy
- Can be stored in an airtight container for up to three days

N.V. : Calories: 85, Fat: 4g, Carbs: 10g, Protein: 5g, Sugar: 0g

RAINBOW CARROT AND ZUCCHINI RIBBONS WITH CHIA SEEDS

PREPARATION TIME: 15 min

COOKING TIME: none

SERVINGS: 2

M.OF COOKING: Raw

INGREDIENTS:

- 3 rainbow carrots, peeled
- 1 zucchini
- 1 lemon, juiced
- 1 Tbls extra-virgin olive oil
- 1 tsp raw honey
- 1 Tbls chia seeds
- Salt and cracked black pepper to taste

DIRECTIONS:

- Use a vegetable peeler to create thin ribbons from the carrots and zucchini
- In a mixing bowl, whisk together lemon juice, olive oil, and honey
- Toss the vegetable ribbons in the dressing, and sprinkle with chia seeds
- Season with salt and pepper to taste, and allow to sit for 10 min for the flavors to meld

TIPS:

- Serve immediately for the crispest texture
- The honey can be replaced with agave for a vegan option

N.V. : Calories: 120, Fat: 7g, Carbs: 14g, Protein: 3g, Sugar: 9g

SPICY EDAMAME WITH STAR ANISE AND SICHUAN PEPPER

PREPARATION TIME: 10 min

COOKING TIME: 5 min

SERVINGS: 4

M.OF COOKING: Sautéing

INGREDIENTS:

- 16 oz. edamame, in the pod
- 1 Tbls sesame oil
- 1 star anise
- ½ tsp Sichuan peppercorns, crushed
- 2 garlic cloves, minced
- Pinch of sea salt
- 1 tsp red pepper flakes

DIRECTIONS:

- Heat the sesame oil in a skillet over medium heat
- Add star anise, Sichuan peppercorns, and garlic, sautéing until fragrant, about 2 min
- Add edamame and sauté for another 3 min
- Season with sea salt and red pepper flakes
- Serve warm or at room temperature

TIPS:

- Remove star anise before serving
- Adjust the spice level by increasing or decreasing red pepper flakes

N.V. : Calories: 190, Fat: 8g, Carbs: 15g, Protein: 17g, Sugar: 3g

5.2 NUTRITIOUS DIPS AND SPREADS

Dive into a world where snacking becomes an opportunity to nourish and delight with our chapter on "Nutritious Dips and Spreads." Gone are the days of feeling guilty about between-meal bites. Instead, we invite you to explore an array of spreads that are as vibrant and healthful as they are simple to whip up. With ingredients that span from creamy avocados and rich nuts to sun-ripened tomatoes and aromatic herbs, these dips and spreads are designed to elevate your snack game to a nutritional masterpiece. Whether you're craving something zesty to liven up your vegetable platter, or a sweet, nut-butter delight to pair with apple slices, each recipe is a testament to the fact that health-forward eating can also be indulgent and satisfying. Let's transform your kitchen counter into a hub of whole-food wonders, where every scoop and smear is an act of self-care.

ROASTED CARROT HUMMUS

PREPARATION TIME: 15 min

COOKING TIME: 25 min

SERVINGS: 6

M.OF COOKING: Baking

INGREDIENTS:

- 1 lb. carrots, peeled and diced
- 3 Tbls extra virgin olive oil, divided
- 1 tsp ground cumin
- 1 tsp smoked paprika
- 2 garlic cloves, minced
- 1 C. canned chickpeas, drained and rinsed
- 2 Tbls tahini
- 4 Tbls fresh lemon juice
- Salt and pepper to taste
- Fresh parsley for garnish

DIRECTIONS:

- Preheat oven to 425°F (220°C)
- Toss carrots with 1 Tbls olive oil, cumin, smoked paprika, and roast until tender
- In a food processor, blend roasted carrots, remaining olive oil, garlic, chickpeas, tahini, lemon juice, salt, and pepper until smooth
- Garnish with parsley

TIPS:

- Roast additional garlic with the carrots for stronger flavor
- Top with sesame seeds for added texture
- If too thick, adjust consistency with a little water

N.V. : Calories: 180, Fat: 10g, Carbs: 20g, Protein: 4g, Sugar: 5g

BEET AND WALNUT PÂTÉ

PREPARATION TIME: 20 min

COOKING TIME: none

SERVINGS: 8

M.OF COOKING: No Cooking

INGREDIENTS:

- 2 medium beets, cooked and peeled
- 1 C. walnuts, toasted
- 1 small red onion, finely chopped
- 1 garlic clove
- 2 Tbls balsamic vinegar
- 1 Tbls extra virgin olive oil
- Fresh thyme leaves
- Salt and pepper to taste
- Crumbled goat cheese for serving

DIRECTIONS:

- Puree beets, walnuts, red onion, garlic, balsamic vinegar, olive oil, thyme, salt, and pepper in a food processor until mixture achieves a pâté consistency

- Serve chilled with a sprinkle of goat cheese

TIPS:

- Toast walnuts mildly to avoid bitterness
- Serve with whole grain crackers for additional fiber
- Can be refrigerated for up to 5 days

N.V. : Calories: 140, Fat: 11g, Carbs: 8g, Protein: 3g, Sugar: 5g

SPICY AVOCADO AND CHIA GUACAMOLE

PREPARATION TIME: 10 min

COOKING TIME: none

SERVINGS: 4

M.OF COOKING: No Cooking

INGREDIENTS:

- 2 ripe avocados
- 1 small jalapeño, minced
- 1 medium tomato, diced
- ¼ C. red onion, finely chopped
- 2 Tbls chia seeds
- 2 Tbls fresh lime juice
- Salt and pepper to taste
- Fresh cilantro, chopped

DIRECTIONS:

- Mash avocados in a bowl
- Stir in jalapeño, tomato, onion, chia seeds, lime juice, salt, and pepper until well combined
- Top with fresh cilantro

TIPS:

- Let the guacamole sit for 10 minutes before serving to allow chia seeds to swell
- Add more lime juice if preferred for a tangier flavor
- Scoop with vegetable sticks for an even healthier option

N.V. : Calories: 200, Fat: 15g, Carbs: 15g, Protein: 4g, Sugar: 2g

MISO AUBERGINE SPREAD

PREPARATION TIME: 15 min

COOKING TIME: 10 min

SERVINGS: 4

M.OF COOKING: Roasting

INGREDIENTS:

- 2 large aubergines
- 2 Tbls white miso paste
- 1 Tbls tahini
- 1 tsp ginger, grated
- 2 tsp tamari or soy sauce
- 1 Tbls rice wine vinegar
- 1 tsp sesame oil
- 1 Tbls honey
- Green onions and black sesame seeds for garnish

DIRECTIONS:

- Preheat grill to high
- Halve aubergines lengthwise, score flesh in a diamond pattern
- Grill aubergines until tender
- Scoop out flesh and blend with miso, tahini, ginger, tamari, vinegar, sesame oil, honey until smooth
- Garnish with green onions, sesame seeds

TIPS:

- Adjust miso quantity according to taste for saltiness
- Can be served warm or cold
- Pairs well with sourdough bread or as a unique sauce for noodles

N.V. : Calories: 120, Fat: 7g, Carbs: 13g, Protein: 3g, Sugar: 7g

SUN-DRIED TOMATO AND CANNELLINI BEAN DIP

PREPARATION TIME: 10 min

COOKING TIME: none

SERVINGS: 6

M.OF COOKING: No Cooking

INGREDIENTS:

- 1 C. cannellini beans, drained and rinsed
- ⅓ C. sun-dried tomatoes in oil, drained
- 2 Tbls fresh basil leaves
- 1 Tbls capers
- 1 garlic clove
- 2 Tbls extra virgin olive oil
- 1 Tbls lemon juice
- Salt and pepper to taste
- Grated Parmesan cheese for serving

DIRECTIONS:

- Blend cannellini beans, sun-dried tomatoes, basil, capers, garlic, olive oil, and lemon juice in a food processor until smooth
- Season with salt, pepper
- Serve sprinkled with Parmesan cheese

TIPS:

- Add a pinch of chili flakes for extra heat
- If the dip is too thick, thin with a small amount of water or additional lemon juice
- Stir in some roasted red peppers for a sweeter dip

N.V. : Calories: 110, Fat: 5g, Carbs: 13g, Protein: 5g, Sugar: 2g

LEMONY ARTICHOKE AND HERB DIP

PREPARATION TIME: 15 min

COOKING TIME: none

SERVINGS: 5

M.OF COOKING: No Cooking

INGREDIENTS:

- 1 C. canned artichoke hearts, drained
- 1 C. Greek yogurt
- 1 Tbls Dijon mustard
- 1 lemon, zested and juiced
- 2 Tbls fresh parsley, chopped
- 1 Tbls fresh dill, chopped
- 1 Tbls chives, chopped
- Salt and pepper to taste

DIRECTIONS:

- Puree artichoke hearts, Greek yogurt, Dijon mustard, lemon zest, and juice in a food processor until smooth
- Stir in parsley, dill, chives, salt, and pepper by hand

TIPS:

- Can be served as a dip or a creamy sauce for roasted vegetables
- Using full-fat Greek yogurt provides a richer texture
- Lemon zest adds a fragrant zing that complements the artichokes beautifully

N.V. : Calories: 90, Fat: 2g, Carbs: 13g, Protein: 5g, Sugar: 3g

PUMPKIN SEED AND CILANTRO PESTO

PREPARATION TIME: 10 min

COOKING TIME: none

SERVINGS: 8

M.OF COOKING: No Cooking

INGREDIENTS:

- 1 C. raw pumpkin seeds, toasted
- 2 C. fresh cilantro leaves, stems removed
- 1 garlic clove
- ½ C. Parmesan cheese, grated
- ½ C. extra virgin olive oil
- 1 lime, juiced
- Salt and pepper to taste

DIRECTIONS:

- Blend pumpkin seeds, cilantro, garlic, Parmesan in a food processor until crumbly

- With the motor running, slowly add olive oil and lime juice until desired consistency is reached
- Season with salt and pepper

TIPS:
- Replace Parmesan with nutritional yeast for a vegan option

- Pesto can be frozen in ice-cube trays for future use
- For a nuttier flavor, add a handful of toasted pecans

N.V. : Calories: 220, Fat: 20g, Carbs: 5g, Protein: 7g, Sugar: 0g

5.3 WHOLE GRAIN AND SEED CRACKERS

In your quest for wholesome nourishment, you might have wondered, "What can I munch on that's both satisfying and in tune with my whole food values?" Our journey through the pantry of nature brings us to a delightful answer: whole grain and seed crackers. These crunchy companions to your dips and spreads are not only easy to make but are bursting with nutritional goodness, offering a fiber-rich snack that supports your well-being. Imagine the delightful poppy seeds speckled across a golden canvas, sunflower seeds adding a nutty depth, and flaxseeds woven in for that omega-3 boost – each cracker is a mosaic of natural ingredients, tailored by your hand to fit every palate at home. Let's roll out these seeds of change together and transform snack time into a delightful ritual that harmonizes your body with the pure rhythms of the earth.

MULTIGRAIN ROSEMARY AND SEA SALT CRACKERS

PREPARATION TIME: 15 min
COOKING TIME: 25 min
SERVINGS: 30
M.OF COOKING: Baking
INGREDIENTS:
- 1 C. whole wheat flour
- 1/2 C. buckwheat flour
- 1/2 C. millet flour
- 1 Tbls flaxseed, ground
- 2 Tbls sunflower seeds
- 1 tsp fresh rosemary, minced
- 1 Tbls extra-virgin olive oil
- 3/4 C. water
- Sea salt flakes for topping

DIRECTIONS:

- Combine flours, ground flaxseed, sunflower seeds, and rosemary in a large bowl
- Add olive oil and water and mix until a dough forms
- Roll dough onto a baking sheet lined with parchment paper until thin
- Score into squares
- Sprinkle with sea salt flakes
- Bake in preheated oven at 350°F (175°C) until crisp and golden

TIPS:
- Transfer crackers to a wire rack immediately after baking to maintain crispness
- Store in an airtight container to preserve freshness

N.V. : Calories: 58, Fat: 2g, Carbs: 9g, Protein: 2g, Sugar: 0g

SESAME SPELT CRACKERS

PREPARATION TIME: 20 min

COOKING TIME: 20 min

SERVINGS: 24

M.OF COOKING: Baking

INGREDIENTS:

- 1 1/2 C. spelt flour
- 1/4 C. sesame seeds
- 1 tsp paprika
- 1/4 tsp garlic powder
- 1/2 tsp sea salt
- 1/4 tsp black pepper
- 4 Tbls cold-pressed coconut oil
- 1/2 C. water

DIRECTIONS:

- In a mixing bowl, combine spelt flour, sesame seeds, paprika, garlic powder, salt, and pepper
- Cut in coconut oil until mixture resembles coarse crumbs
- Gradually add water to form a firm dough
- Roll out on a floured surface; cut into shapes
- Bake at 375°F (190°C) until edges are lightly browned

TIPS:

- Keep dough covered with a damp cloth to prevent drying out while working
- Optional: Toast sesame seeds lightly before adding to the mix for enhanced flavor

N.V. : Calories: 70, Fat: 4g, Carbs: 7g, Protein: 2g, Sugar: 0g

QUINOA CHIA SEED CRACKERS

PREPARATION TIME: 10 min

COOKING TIME: 30 min

SERVINGS: 25

M.OF COOKING: Baking

INGREDIENTS:

- 1 C. quinoa flour
- 1/4 C. chia seeds
- 1/2 tsp Himalayan pink salt
- 1/4 tsp cracked black pepper
- 1 Tbls cold-pressed olive oil
- 1/3 C. water

DIRECTIONS:

- Stir together quinoa flour, chia seeds, salt, and pepper in a bowl
- Add oil and water, mix until a dough forms
- Roll out on parchment paper to 1/4 inch thick
- Cut into squares or desired shapes
- Bake at 350°F (175°C) until crispy

TIPS:

- For extra crunch, let the dough sit for 10 minutes before rolling to allow chia seeds to swell
- These are great served with a bean dip or guacamole

N.V. : Calories: 45, Fat: 2.5g, Carbs: 5g, Protein: 1g, Sugar: 0g

HERBED OAT AND TEFF CRACKERS

PREPARATION TIME: 12 min

COOKING TIME: 22 min

SERVINGS: 20

M.OF COOKING: Baking

INGREDIENTS:

- 3/4 C. oat flour
- 1/2 C. teff flour
- 1 Tbls dried thyme
- 1 Tbls dried oregano
- 1/2 tsp unrefined sea salt
- 3 Tbls extra virgin olive oil
- 1/2 C. warm water

DIRECTIONS:

- Whisk together oat and teff flours, thyme, oregano, and salt

- Drizzle in olive oil and add warm water to form a pliable dough
- Roll out thinly between two sheets of parchment, remove top sheet
- Cut into desired shapes
- Bake in preheated oven at 350°F (175°C) until slightly golden and firm to the touch

TIPS:

- Herbs can be adjusted to suit taste preferences or replaced with Italian seasoning for a different flavor profile
- Perfect paired with a robust cheese or a smear of tapenade

N.V. : Calories: 60, Fat: 3g, Carbs: 8g, Protein: 1g, Sugar: 0g

PUMPKIN SEED AMARANTH CRACKERS

PREPARATION TIME: 18 min
COOKING TIME: 15 min
SERVINGS: 40
M.OF COOKING: Baking
INGREDIENTS:

- 1 C. amaranth flour
- 1/3 C. pumpkin seeds, roughly chopped
- 1/4 tsp cayenne pepper
- 1/2 tsp sea salt
- 2 Tbls avocado oil
- 1/2 C. water

DIRECTIONS:

- Combine amaranth flour, chopped pumpkin seeds, cayenne pepper, and sea salt in a bowl
- Mix in avocado oil and water to create a firm dough
- Roll out dough thinly on a baking tray lined with parchment
- Score into rectangles
- Bake at 375°F (190°C) for a crisp texture

TIPS:

- Toasting pumpkin seeds before adding to the dough can enhance their nutty flavor
- Can be enjoyed solo or as an accompaniment to soups and salads

N.V. : Calories: 55, Fat: 3g, Carbs: 6g, Protein: 2g, Sugar: 0g

BARLEY AND POPPY SEED SNAP CRACKERS

PREPARATION TIME: 10 min
COOKING TIME: 20 min
SERVINGS: 32
M.OF COOKING: Baking
INGREDIENTS:

- 3/4 C. barley flour
- 1/4 C. brown rice flour
- 2 Tbls poppy seeds
- 1/2 tsp coarse sea salt
- 1 Tbls melted grass-fed butter
- 1/2 C. boiling water

DIRECTIONS:

- In a medium bowl, blend barley and brown rice flours with poppy seeds and salt
- Stir in melted butter and boiling water until a cohesive dough forms
- Flatten the dough on a baking sheet to an even thickness
- Cut into squares and prick with a fork
- Bake at 400°F (200°C) until golden

TIPS:

- Keep a close eye during baking as these crackers can go from perfectly done to overdone quickly
- Store in a cool, dry place to retain snap and freshness

N.V. : Calories: 48, Fat: 1.5g, Carbs: 8g, Protein: 1g, Sugar: 0g

BLACK SESAME AND NORI CRACKERS

PREPARATION TIME: 12 min

COOKING TIME: 15 min

SERVINGS: 36

M.OF COOKING: Baking

INGREDIENTS:

- 1 C. almond flour
- 1/2 C. tapioca starch
- 2 Tbls black sesame seeds
- 2 sheets nori seaweed, finely chopped
- 1 tsp sea salt
- 3 Tbls sesame oil
- 1/4 C. water

DIRECTIONS:

- Combine the almond flour, tapioca starch, black sesame seeds, nori, and salt in a large bowl
- Add sesame oil and water, and knead until dough forms
- Roll out between two sheets of baking paper to 1/8 inch thickness
- Cut into diamond shapes
- Bake at 350°F (175°C) until crisp

TIPS:

- For a more intense flavor, lightly toast the black sesame seeds before adding to the mix
- These are delightful when paired with a tangy rice vinegar dipping sauce

N.V. : Calories: 65, Fat: 4.5g, Carbs: 5g, Protein: 2g, Sugar: 0g

CHAPTER 6: FERMENTED FOODS AND GUT HEALTH

6.1 INTRODUCTION TO FERMENTED FOODS

Welcome to the world of fermented foods, a treasure trove of taste and tradition that weaves a rich tapestry of gut-friendly benefits. Fermentation, one of the oldest forms of food preservation, is a delicate dance of time, temperature, and beneficial bacteria. With each jar of homemade sauerkraut and every batch of kefir, we unlock a symphony of flavors and a powerhouse of probiotics that adorn our plates and bolster our bodily wellbeing.

In this chapter, we'll embark on a journey through the art and science of fermented foods. We'll explore how these tangy, zestful edibles don't just punch up our palates—they epitomize nature's wisdom by enhancing our gastrointestinal flora, which is the cornerstone of robust health. You'll discover how to nurture these living foods in your own kitchen, and how, with a little patience and care, they can transform meals into vibrant, health-giving experiences—nourishment truly befitting a temple.

CLASSIC SAUERKRAUT

PREPARATION TIME: 20 min

COOKING TIME: 3-4 weeks fermentation

SERVINGS: 10

M.OF COOKING: Fermentation

INGREDIENTS:

- 1 medium head green cabbage, shredded
- 1.5 Tbls kosher or sea salt
- 1 Tbls caraway seeds

DIRECTIONS:

- Combine cabbage and salt in a large mixing bowl
- Massage the salt into the cabbage until juices are released
- Mix in caraway seeds
- Pack mixture into a large glass jar, pressing down firmly until the cabbage is submerged in its own liquid
- Cover the jar with a clean cloth and secure with a rubber band
- Let the jar sit at room temperature, away from direct sunlight, for 3-4 weeks, checking periodically to ensure cabbage remains submerged

TIPS:

- Taste your sauerkraut after 3 weeks to check for desired tartness
- If mold forms on the surface, skim it off - the sauerkraut beneath is still safe to eat

- Store fully fermented sauerkraut in the refrigerator

N.V. : Calories: 27, Fat: 0.1g, Carbs: 6.7g, Protein: 1.3g, Sugar: 3.4g

BEET KVASS

PREPARATION TIME: 10 min

COOKING TIME: 10-14 days fermentation

SERVINGS: 8 pt.

M.OF COOKING: Fermentation

INGREDIENTS:

- 4 medium beets, cubed
- 1 Tbls sea salt
- Filtered water to fill a gallon jar
- Optional: orange slices, ginger root slices

DIRECTIONS:

- Place beet cubes at the bottom of a clean gallon jar
- Add optional flavorings like orange slices or ginger root slices if desired
- Pour in filtered water, leaving 1-inch headspace at the top
- Stir in sea salt until dissolved
- Cover the jar with a cloth and secure with a rubber band
- Allow the mixture to ferment at room temperature, out of direct sunlight for 10-14 days

TIPS:

- Check daily to ensure beets are submerged in the liquid
- Start tasting kvass after 7 days to find the fermentation sweet spot
- Once fermented, refrigerate to slow fermentation

N.V. : Calories: 44, Fat: 0.2g, Carbs: 10g, Protein: 1.6g, Sugar: 7.8g

GARLIC AND DILL LACTO-FERMENTED PICKLES

PREPARATION TIME: 30 min

COOKING TIME: 4-6 days fermentation

SERVINGS: 5

M.OF COOKING: Fermentation

INGREDIENTS:

- 4 lb. pickling cucumbers, washed
- 1 bunch fresh dill
- 6 cloves garlic, peeled and crushed
- 6 dried bay leaves
- 1 Tbls black peppercorns
- 3 Tbls kosher or pickling salt
- ½ gallon filtered water
- Oak or grape leaves (optional, for crispness)

DIRECTIONS:

- Combine salt and water in a pitcher to make a brine, stirring until salt is dissolved
- In a large crock or glass jar, layer cucumbers with dill, garlic, bay leaves, peppercorns, and optional oak or grape leaves
- Pour brine over the cucumbers, ensuring they are completely submerged
- Place a fermentation weight over the cucumbers to keep them submerged
- Cover the container with a cloth and let it ferment at room temperature for 4-6 days

TIPS:

- If scum forms on the surface, remove it with a spoon
- Taste pickles daily starting on day 4 to achieve desired flavor
- Refrigerate to halt fermentation once pickles reach your preferred sourness

N.V. : Calories: 12, Fat: 0.1g, Carbs: 2.8g, Protein: 0.6g, Sugar: 1.3g

HOMEMADE KIMCHI

PREPARATION TIME: 45 min

COOKING TIME: 1 week fermentation

SERVINGS: 8

M.OF COOKING: Fermentation

INGREDIENTS:

- 2 heads Napa cabbage, chopped
- ½ C. sea salt
- 12 cups water
- 1 daikon radish, grated
- 4 scallions, sliced
- ½ cup Korean red pepper flakes (gochugaru)
- ¼ cup fish sauce
- ¼ cup minced garlic
- 2 tsp sugar
- 2 tsp grated ginger

DIRECTIONS:

- Dissolve sea salt in water to create a brine and soak the chopped Napa cabbage for about 4 hours
- Drain cabbage and rinse under cold water
- In a separate bowl, mix radish, scallions, gochugaru, fish sauce, garlic, sugar, and ginger to form a paste
- Massage paste into cabbage until thoroughly coated
- Pack cabbage into a jar, pressing down firmly to eliminate air bubbles
- Leave at least 1-inch of space at the top of the jar
- Seal the jar and allow it to ferment at room temperature for 1 week

TIPS:

- Monitor kimchi for gas buildup and burp jars if necessary
- Ensure cabbage remains submerged to prevent mold
- Refrigerate after fermenting to your liking to preserve flavor and crunch

N.V. : Calories: 40, Fat: 1g, Carbs: 7g, Protein: 2g, Sugar: 3g

---

FERMENTED CHILI SAUCE

PREPARATION TIME: 20 min

COOKING TIME: 7 days fermentation

SERVINGS: 16 fl. oz.

M.OF COOKING: Fermentation

INGREDIENTS:

- 1 lb. red chili peppers, stemmed and halved
- 6 cloves garlic, peeled
- 2 tsp sea salt
- 2 cups unchlorinated water
- 1 Tbls raw sugar
-

DIRECTIONS:

- Blend chili peppers, garlic, and raw sugar in a food processor until a coarse mash forms
- Dissolve sea salt in the water to create a brine
- Combine pepper mash with brine in a large jar, making sure the peppers are submerged in the liquid
- Cover with a cloth and secure with a rubber band
- Let the mixture ferment at room temperature for 7 days, stirring once a day to prevent mold from forming.
- Store in the refrigerator to slow the fermentation process

TIPS:

- Mix well before each use to blend flavors
- The sauce can continue to ferment and develop flavor in the refrigerator
- If too spicy, dilute with additional brine or vinegar

N.V. : Calories: 23, Fat: 0.4g, Carbs: 4.8g, Protein: 1g, Sugar: 2.8g

---

PRESERVED LEMONS

PREPARATION TIME: 10 min

COOKING TIME: 30 days fermentation

SERVINGS: 12

M. OF COOKING: Fermentation

INGREDIENTS:

- 5-6 organic lemons, scrubbed clean
- 6 Tbls sea salt
- Optional spices: 1 cinnamon stick, 5 cloves, 1 bay leaf
- Freshly squeezed lemon juice, if necessary to cover

DIRECTIONS:

- Quarter the lemons from the top to within ½ inch of the bottom, sprinkle salt on the exposed flesh, then reshape the fruit
- Place 1 tablespoon salt on the bottom of a sterilized jar
- Pack in the lemons and add any optional spices
- Press the lemons down to release their juices and to make room for the remaining lemons
- If the juice released from the squeezed lemons does not cover them, add freshly squeezed lemon juice until they are covered
- Leave some air space before sealing the jar
- Let the lemons ripen at room temperature for 30 days, turning the jar upside down occasionally

TIPS:

- Wash lemons before using to remove salt
- Once opened, preserved lemons should be kept in the refrigerator
- The preserved lemons can be used in a variety of dishes, from tagines to dressings

N.V. : Calories: 25, Fat: 0g, Carbs: 8g, Protein: 0.3g, Sugar: 2.5g

---

GINGERED CARROT KRAUT

PREPARATION TIME: 30 min

COOKING TIME: 3-4 weeks fermentation

SERVINGS: 8

M. OF COOKING: Fermentation

INGREDIENTS:

- 2 lb carrots, peeled and grated
- 2 inch piece of ginger, finely grated
- 4 tsp sea salt

DIRECTIONS:

- Mix carrots, ginger, and salt in a large mixing bowl
- Massage the salt into the vegetables until a generous amount of liquid is released
- Pack the mixture into a fermentation crock or wide-mouth jar, pressing down firmly to ensure the vegetables are submerged in their own juices
- Cover the crock with a cloth to keep out dust and let it ferment at room temperature for 3-4 weeks

TIPS:

- Do not use iodized salt as it can inhibit fermentation
- If a white film appears on the surface, simply skim it off; it's a common occurrence in fermenting vegetables
- Tightly sealing the jars and storing them in the refrigerator will slow the fermentation process and preserve the kraut for longer periods

N.V. : Calories: 45, Fat: 0.2g, Carbs: 10.5g, Protein: 1g, Sugar: 5g

6.2 Homemade Sauerkraut and Kimchi

Embracing the ancient wisdom of fermentation, we unlock a world of probiotic potential right in the cozy confines of our kitchens. Imagine the satisfying crunch of tangy sauerkraut and the bold, complex flavor of piquant kimchi as integral parts of your digestive wellness journey. These are not just side dishes—they are cultural staples rich in beneficial bacteria that bolster our gut health and elevate our culinary experience.

In this subchapter, you'll don the hat of a fermentation artisan, learning the simple yet profound art of crafting homemade sauerkraut and kimchi. With each fold of cabbage and sprinkle of salt, you'll be fermenting far more than just food; you're cultivating vitality, flavor, and a joyful balance that resonates from your taste buds to your tummy. Let's turn cabbage into a gut-healing delicacy and enter the flavorful ferment revolution that has spanned centuries and continents. Happy fermenting!

CLASSIC CABBAGE SAUERKRAUT

PREPARATION TIME: 15 min.

COOKING TIME: 2-4 weeks fermentation

SERVINGS: 4 qt.

M.OF COOKING: Fermentation

INGREDIENTS:

- 1 medium head green cabbage, finely shredded
- 1 Tbls caraway seeds
- 2 Tbls sea salt
- Spring water, as needed to cover

DIRECTIONS:

- Remove outer leaves of cabbage and set aside
- Slice cabbage finely and place in a large mixing bowl
- Massage salt into cabbage for about 10 minutes to release juices
- Mix in caraway seeds
- Pack mixture tightly into a fermentation crock
- Pour spring water to cover cabbage if needed, cabbage should be submerged
- Place whole cabbage leaves on top to keep mixture submerged below the brine
- Seal crock and allow to ferment at room temperature out of direct sunlight for 2-4 weeks

TIPS:

- Monitor brine level throughout fermentation, ensuring cabbage remains submerged
- Taste sauerkraut every few days until desired sourness is reached
- Once fermentation is complete, sauerkraut can be stored in the refrigerator for several months

N.V. : Calories: 27, Fat: 0.1g, Carbs: 6.7g, Protein: 1.3g, Sugar: 3.4g

RUBY RED KRAUT WITH JUNIPER BERRIES

PREPARATION TIME: 20 min.

COOKING TIME: 4-6 weeks fermentation

SERVINGS: 3 qt.

M.OF COOKING: Fermentation

INGREDIENTS:

- 1 large red cabbage, core removed and leaves finely shredded
- 1 Tbls juniper berries
- 2 Tbls Himalayan pink salt
- 1 tsp caraway seeds

- Filtered water to cover, as needed

DIRECTIONS:

- In a large bowl, massage pink salt into shredded red cabbage until it begins to soften and release liquid
- Crush juniper berries lightly to release flavors and add to the cabbage along with caraway seeds
- Pack mixture into a fermentation vessel, pressing down firmly to remove air pockets
- Add filtered water to ensure cabbage is fully submerged under the brine
- Cover with cabbage leaves and weigh down to keep submerged
- Allow to sit at moderate room temperature, out of direct sunlight, for a period of 4-6 weeks

TIPS:

- Inspect regularly to ensure cabbage remains submerged below brine
- If any mold forms on the surface, remove promptly and ensure the kraut is still covered by brine
- Upon reaching desired tartness and flavor, transfer to refrigerator to halt fermentation

N.V. : Calories: 29, Fat: 0g, Carbs: 6.9g, Protein: 1.4g, Sugar: 3.8g

GINGER TURMERIC SAUERKRAUT

PREPARATION TIME: 20 min.
COOKING TIME: 3 weeks fermentation
SERVINGS: 8 C.
M. OF COOKING: Fermentation
INGREDIENTS:

- 2 medium heads green cabbage, finely shredded
- 4-inch piece of fresh ginger, grated
- 1 Tbls ground turmeric
- 1 Tbls sea salt

- Distilled water to cover, as needed

DIRECTIONS:

- Begin by shredding cabbage into a large bowl, sprinkle with sea salt, and knead vigorously until brine starts to form
- Grate ginger finely and mix with ground turmeric
- Combine ginger and turmeric mixture with cabbage
- Tightly pack into a fermentation vessel, making sure to release any air bubbles
- Cover with distilled water so that cabbage is entirely submerged under the brine
- Place whole cabbage leaves on top, then weigh down to ensure cabbage stays under the liquid
- Cover vessel and allow to ferment at room temperature for about 3 weeks

TIPS:

- During fermentation, be sure to check that cabbage remains covered by brine to prevent unwanted mold
- The ginger-turmeric combination may cause the sauerkraut to become more vibrant in color
- Transfer to fridge to preserve once preferred level of sourness is reached

N.V. : Calories: 35, Fat: 0.2g, Carbs: 8.1g, Protein: 1.7g, Sugar: 4.2g

SPICY KOREAN KIMCHI

PREPARATION TIME: 30 min.
COOKING TIME: 1-2 weeks fermentation
SERVINGS: 2 qt.
M. OF COOKING: Fermentation
INGREDIENTS:

- 1 Napa cabbage, quartered and chopped
- 1/4 C. sea salt
- 1 Tbls grated garlic
- 1 Tbls grated ginger

- 1 tsp sugar
- 3 Tbls water
- 1-5 Tbls Korean red pepper flakes (gochugaru)
- 1 daikon radish, peeled and cut into matchsticks
- 4 green onions, sliced
- Fish sauce, to taste (optional for added umami flavor)

DIRECTIONS:
- Separate Napa cabbage leaves and sprinkle each layer with sea salt
- Set aside for 2 hours to allow salt to draw out moisture
- Rinse cabbage thoroughly and drain
- In a large bowl, create a paste with garlic, ginger, sugar, water, and gochugaru to taste
- Add chopped daikon and green onions to the paste and toss gently
- Coat each cabbage leaf with the mixture
- Pack kimchi into a fermentation container, pressing down to eliminate air pockets and top with enough water to cover
- Cover the container and let it ferment at room temperature for 1-2 weeks, depending on desired sourness

TIPS:
- Each day, press down on kimchi to keep it submerged in its juices
- Rinse off any white mold that may form, this is often harmless but keep area clean
- Kimchi will continue to ferment in the refrigerator and can be enjoyed for several months

N.V. : Calories: 23, Fat: 0.3g, Carbs: 4.1g, Protein: 1.0g, Sugar: 2.0g

CLASSIC HOMEMADE SAUERKRAUT

PREPARATION TIME: 20 min.

COOKING TIME: 1-4 weeks fermenting

SERVINGS: 1 gallon

M.OF COOKING: Fermentation

INGREDIENTS:
- 5 lb. shredded green cabbage
- 3 Tbls sea salt
- 1 Tbls caraway seeds
- Distilled water as needed to cover cabbage

DIRECTIONS:
- Massage cabbage and salt together until moist and wilted
- Pack mixture tightly into a sterilized fermentation crock, sprinkling in caraway seeds as you go
- Ensure the cabbage is fully submerged under its liquid, adding additional saltwater solution if necessary (1 tsp of salt per 1 C. of water)
- Seal crock or cover with airtight lid fitted with airlock, and store at room temperature away from direct sunlight for 1-4 weeks, checking regularly and skimming off any scum that may form
- Taste periodically until desired flavor is achieved, then refrigerate to stop fermentation

TIPS:
- Keep veggies submerged to prevent mold
- Use a glass weight or a clean stone to keep cabbage submerged under brine
- Taste test at one week for flavor and texture preferences

N.V. : Calories: 27, Fat: 0.1g, Carbs: 6.1g, Protein: 1.3g, Sugar: 3.3g

SPICY AUTHENTIC KIMCHI

PREPARATION TIME: 30 min.

COOKING TIME: 1 week fermenting

SERVINGS: 2 quarts

M.OF COOKING: Fermentation

INGREDIENTS:

- 2 medium napa cabbages, cut into squares
- ½ C. sea salt
- Water to cover cabbage
- 1 Tbls grated ginger
- 4 cloves garlic, minced
- 1 tsp sugar
- 3 Tbls fish sauce
- 5 Tbls gochugaru (Korean red pepper powder)
- 8 oz. Korean radish or daikon, peeled and matchstick-cut
- 4 scallions, trimmed and cut into 1-inch pieces

DIRECTIONS:

- Dissolve sea salt in enough water to cover cabbages and let them sit for 2 hours, turning every 30 min.
- Rinse cabbage under cold water and drain
- Make paste by combining garlic, ginger, sugar, fish sauce, and gochugaru in a bowl
- Add radish and scallions to the paste
- Gently, but thoroughly, massage the paste into the cabbage leaves
- Pack mixture into a sterilized fermentation jar, pressing down to eliminate air pockets and leaving at least 1 inch of space at the top
- Seal the jar with an airtight lid fitted with an airlock
- Ferment for 5-7 days at room temperature, out of direct sunlight
- When bubbles stop rising, and the kimchi tastes tart, transfer to the refrigerator

TIPS:

- If the kimchi is too spicy, reduce the gochugaru
- To make it vegetarian, substitute fish sauce with kelp powder mixed with water

- If mold develops on the surface, simply skim it off; the kimchi beneath should still be safe to eat

N.V. : Calories: 23, Fat: 0.5g, Carbs: 4g, Protein: 2g, Sugar: 2g

BEETROOT AND RED CABBAGE SAUERKRAUT

PREPARATION TIME: 25 min.
COOKING TIME: 3-6 weeks fermenting
SERVINGS: 1 gallon
M.OF COOKING: Fermentation
INGREDIENTS:

- 3 lb. red cabbage, finely shredded
- 2 lb. beetroots, peeled and grated
- 3 Tbls sea salt
- 1 Tbls juniper berries
- 1 qt. distilled water

DIRECTIONS:

- Combine red cabbage, beetroots, and sea salt in a large bowl, mashing with your hands to release juices
- Mix in juniper berries
- Pack mixture into a sterilized fermentation crock, ensuring it is submerged under its juices
- If necessary, add a saltwater solution (1 tsp of salt per 1 qt. of water) to cover the vegetables
- Seal crock or cover with airtight lid and airlock, and allow to ferment at room temperature, out of direct sunlight, checking and skimming any scum that forms
- After 3 weeks, start tasting; once it reaches a tangy flavor to your liking, transfer to the refrigerator to halt fermentation

TIPS:

- Juniper berries add a distinct aromatic note

- Beetroot stains; wear gloves to avoid pink hands
- The vibrant color of this sauerkraut brings a pop to any plate

N.V. : Calories: 38, Fat: 0.2g, Carbs: 8.2g, Protein: 1.7g, Sugar: 5.3g

6.3 KEFIR AND YOGURT BASICS

In the tapestry of whole food nutrition, the delicate threads of fermented delights, such as kefir and yogurt, are essential for weaving a robust gut health narrative. These ancient foods, cultured companions for our microbiome, are both a nod to tradition and nodal points for wellness. In this chapter, we dip into the creamy world of kefir and yogurt, unpicking the mysteries contained within their live cultures.

Discover the symphony of beneficial bacteria that play within these ferments, learn the simple artistry of crafting them in your own kitchen, and witness the alchemy that transforms the humble milk into tangy, gut-nourishing essentials. Through understanding the basics, you will find that integrating these fermented foods into your daily regimen is not just a nod towards improving digestive health—it's a daily ritual that celebrates the synergy of taste and well-being.

HOMEMADE TRADITIONAL KEFIR

PREPARATION TIME: 24 hrs
COOKING TIME: none
SERVINGS: 4 pt.
M.OF COOKING: Fermentation
INGREDIENTS:
- 4 pt. whole milk
- 1 Tbls kefir grains

DIRECTIONS:
- Pour milk into a clean glass jar
- Stir in kefir grains
- Cover with a breathable cloth secured with a rubber band
- Place in a warm area around 68-78°F (20-25°C) for 24 hrs
- Once milk has thickened and has a tangy flavor, strain out the kefir grains
- Store kefir in the refrigerator

TIPS:

- Use grains obtained from a reliable source for best results
- Incorporate kefir into smoothies for a probiotic boost
- Kefir grains can be reused indefinitely with proper care

N.V. : Calories: 150 per cup, Fat: 8g per cup, Carbs: 12g per cup, Protein: 8g per cup, Sugar: 12g per cup

VANILLA INFUSED KEFIR

PREPARATION TIME: 24 hrs 10 min
COOKING TIME: none
SERVINGS: 4 pt.
M.OF COOKING: Fermentation
INGREDIENTS:
- 4 pt. whole milk
- 1 Tbls kefir grains
- 1 vanilla pod, scored and scraped

DIRECTIONS:

- Follow the same steps as traditional kefir for preparation
- After the fermentation process, before storing, infuse with the vanilla pod and scraped seeds for an additional 10 min
- Strain and chill in the refrigerator
- Remove the vanilla pod before serving

TIPS:

- Vanilla enhances the natural sweetness of kefir without added sugars
- Use the rest of the vanilla pod to infuse sugar or salt

N.V. : Calories: 152 per cup, Fat: 8g per cup, Carbs: 13g per cup, Protein: 8g per cup, Sugar: 13g per cup

COCONUT MILK KEFIR

PREPARATION TIME: 18 hrs

COOKING TIME: none

SERVINGS: 4 pt.

M. OF COOKING: Fermentation

INGREDIENTS:

- 4 pt. full-fat coconut milk
- 1 Tbls water kefir grains

DIRECTIONS:

- Combine coconut milk and water kefir grains in a glass jar
- Cover with a non-reactive lid or cloth
- Let sit at room temperature, away from direct sunlight, for 18 hrs † Strain the grains
- Refrigerate the coconut milk kefir until chilled

TIPS:

- Coconut milk kefir is a great dairy-free alternative
- Make sure to use full-fat coconut milk for a richer texture
- Stir before serving as separation may occur

N.V. : Calories: 450 per cup, Fat: 48g per cup, Carbs: 6g per cup, Protein: 2g per cup, Sugar: 3g per cup

STRAWBERRY KEFIR SMOOTHIE

PREPARATION TIME: 5 min

COOKING TIME: none

SERVINGS: 2

M. OF COOKING: Blending

INGREDIENTS:

- 2 C. kefir
- 1 C. fresh strawberries, hulled
- 1 Tbls honey
- 1 tsp freshly squeezed lemon juice

DIRECTIONS:

- Blend kefir, strawberries, honey, and lemon juice on high speed until smooth
- Serve immediately for a refreshing drink

TIPS:

- For added nutrition, include a tablespoon of chia seeds
- Frozen strawberries can be used instead of fresh for a colder smoothie

N.V. : Calories: 150 per serving, Fat: 4g per serving, Carbs: 20g per serving, Protein: 8g per serving, Sugar: 18g per serving

SAVORY KEFIR HERB DRESSING

PREPARATION TIME: 10 min

COOKING TIME: none

SERVINGS: 1 cup

M. OF COOKING: Mixing

INGREDIENTS:

- ¾ C. kefir
- ¼ C. extra-virgin olive oil
- 1 Tbls fresh dill, finely chopped
- 1 Tbls fresh parsley, finely chopped
- 2 tsp fresh chives, finely chopped
- 1 clove garlic, minced
- Salt and pepper to taste

DIRECTIONS:

- Whisk together kefir and olive oil until smooth
- Add herbs, garlic, salt, and pepper to the mixture
- Whisk until fully combined
- Let sit for a few minutes to allow flavors to meld
- Use as dressing for salads or as a dip for vegetables

TIPS:

- This dressing can be stored in the fridge for up to a week
- Shake well before using if separation occurs

N.V. : Calories: 99 per Tbls, Fat: 10g per Tbls, Carbs: 1g per Tbls, Protein: 1g per Tbls, Sugar: 1g per Tbls

CACAO AND CHIA SEED KEFIR PUDDING

PREPARATION TIME: 5 min

COOKING TIME: none

SERVINGS: 2

M.OF COOKING: No Cooking

INGREDIENTS:

- 2 C. kefir
- 3 Tbls chia seeds
- 2 Tbls raw cacao powder
- 1 Tbls pure maple syrup
- 1 tsp vanilla extract

DIRECTIONS:

- In a bowl, mix together kefir, chia seeds, cacao powder, maple syrup, and vanilla extract
- Stir until well combined
- Let it sit for 5 min. then stir again
- Cover and refrigerate overnight to thicken
- Serve chilled

TIPS:

- This pudding's consistency can be adjusted by adding more or less kefir
- Top with fresh berries or nuts before serving for added texture and flavor

N.V. : Calories: 195 per serving, Fat: 7g per serving, Carbs: 25g per serving, Protein: 11g per serving, Sugar: 14g per serving

GOLDEN KEFIR LATTE

PREPARATION TIME: 10 min

COOKING TIME: none

SERVINGS: 1

M.OF COOKING: Stirring

INGREDIENTS:

- 1 C. kefir
- 1 tsp turmeric powder
- ½ tsp cinnamon
- ¼ tsp ginger powder
- 1 tsp honey
- A pinch of black pepper

DIRECTIONS:

- Heat kefir gently in a saucepan over low heat – do not boil
- Whisk in turmeric, cinnamon, ginger, honey, and black pepper until fully dissolved
- Simmer for a couple of minutes, stirring constantly
- Pour into a mug and enjoy warm

TIPS:

- The black pepper helps to increase the absorption of turmeric's beneficial properties
- Can be enjoyed cold as well
- To make it vegan, substitute honey with agave syrup

N.V. : Calories: 120, Fat: 4g, Carbs: 15g, Protein: 8g, Sugar: 15g

Chapter 7: Healthy Desserts

7.1 Fruit-Based Sweet Treats

Indulge in the natural sweetness of fruits with our myriad of delightful concoctions in sub-chapter 7.1. Imagine transforming the earth's candy into desserts that not only tantalize your taste buds but also nourish your body. In this section, we'll explore simple, yet exquisite recipes that showcase fruit in its purest form. From the vibrant notes of fresh berries to the rich, succulent textures of mangoes and peaches, we're about to turn your kitchen into a canvas for luscious fruit-based masterpieces. Whether you're craving something light and refreshing or decadently sweet, these treats promise satisfaction without the remorse of typical sugary desserts. By harnessing the inherent sweetness of fruit, we'll create desserts that serve not only as a finale to your meals but also as nutritious snacks to energize your day. Let's journey together to sweeten our lives, one fruit at a time.

GRILLED PEACH WITH CINNAMON HONEY DRIZZLE

PREPARATION TIME: 5 min.

COOKING TIME: 5 min.

SERVINGS: 4

M.OF COOKING: Grilling

INGREDIENTS:

- 2 large peaches, halved and pitted
- 1 Tbls coconut oil
- 2 Tbls honey
- ½ tsp ground cinnamon
- 1 tsp fresh lemon juice
- Pinch of sea salt
- Fresh mint leaves for garnish

DIRECTIONS:

- Preheat grill to medium-high heat and brush peach halves with coconut oil
- Place peaches on the grill, cut side down, and cook until charred and tender, about 2-3 min. per side
- In a small bowl, whisk together honey, cinnamon, lemon juice, and sea salt
- Drizzle the honey mixture over the grilled peaches and garnish with mint leaves

TIPS:

- Serve with a dollop of Greek yogurt for added protein
- Can be served with granola for a crunchier texture

N.V. : Calories: 120, Fat: 5g, Carbs: 19g, Protein: 1g, Sugar: 18g

FROZEN BERRY YOGURT BARK

PREPARATION TIME: 15 min.

COOKING TIME: none

SERVINGS: 8

M. OF COOKING: Freezing

INGREDIENTS:

- 2 C. Greek yogurt, plain
- 3 Tbls maple syrup
- 1 tsp vanilla extract
- 1 C. mixed berries (strawberries, blueberries, raspberries), chopped
- 1 Tbls chia seeds
- Zest of 1 lemon

DIRECTIONS:

- Line a baking sheet with parchment paper
- In a bowl, mix Greek yogurt, maple syrup, vanilla extract, and lemon zest until smooth
- Spread the yogurt mixture on the prepared baking sheet, creating a ½-inch thick layer
- Sprinkle the chopped berries and chia seeds over the yogurt layer
- Freeze until solid, about 4 hr. or overnight
- Break into pieces

TIPS:

- Store in an airtight container in the freezer to maintain freshness
- Customizable with nuts or dark chocolate bits for extra flavor

N.V. : Calories: 90, Fat: 2g, Carbs: 13g, Protein: 5g, Sugar: 10g

FIG AND WALNUT STUFFED APPLES

PREPARATION TIME: 15 min.

COOKING TIME: 45 min.

SERVINGS: 6

M. OF COOKING: Baking

INGREDIENTS:

- 6 medium apples, cored
- 12 dried figs, finely chopped
- ½ C. walnuts, chopped
- 2 Tbls honey
- 1 tsp ground cardamom
- ½ tsp ground nutmeg
- ¼ C. apple cider
- 1 Tbls lemon juice

DIRECTIONS:

- Preheat oven to 350°F (175°C)
- In a bowl, combine figs, walnuts, honey, cardamom, and nutmeg
- Stuff each apple with the fig mixture
- Place stuffed apples in a baking dish
- Mix apple cider with lemon juice and pour into the dish around the apples
- Cover with foil and bake until apples are soft, about 45 min.

TIPS:

- Serve with a scoop of vanilla ice cream or coconut whipped cream for extra indulgence
- Leftovers can be chopped and added to oatmeal or salads

N.V. : Calories: 210, Fat: 7g, Carbs: 39g, Protein: 2g, Sugar: 30g

PAPAYA LIME SORBET

PREPARATION TIME: 20 min.

COOKING TIME: none

SERVINGS: 4

M. OF COOKING: Freezing

INGREDIENTS:

- 1 large papaya, peeled, seeded, and chopped
- Juice of 2 limes
- Zest of 1 lime
- ¼ C. honey
- Pinch of sea salt

DIRECTIONS:

- In a food processor, blend chopped papaya, lime juice, lime zest, honey, and sea salt until smooth
- Pour the mixture into a freezer-safe container and freeze until firm, about 3-4 hr.

- Once frozen, scrape with a fork to create a fluffy texture

TIPS:

- Adding a splash of coconut water can enhance tropical flavors
- Serve immediately after scraping for the best texture

N.V. : Calories: 145, Fat: 0.3g, Carbs: 37g, Protein: 0.6g, Sugar: 34g

AVOCADO CHOCOLATE MOUSSE WITH RASPBERRIES

PREPARATION TIME: 10 min.

COOKING TIME: none

SERVINGS: 2

M.OF COOKING: Blending

INGREDIENTS:

- 1 ripe avocado
- 2 Tbls cocoa powder, unsweetened
- 2 Tbls maple syrup
- ½ tsp pure vanilla extract
- ¼ C. almond milk, unsweetened
- ½ C. raspberries for topping

DIRECTIONS:

- Scoop out the avocado flesh and place in a blender
- Add cocoa powder, maple syrup, vanilla extract, and almond milk
- Blend until smooth and creamy
- Chill for at least 1 hr.
- Top with fresh raspberries before serving

TIPS:

- For a richer texture, blend in a tablespoon of almond butter
- Experiment with sweeteners like honey or agave nectar to suit your taste

N.V. : Calories: 250, Fat: 15g, Carbs: 31g, Protein: 4g, Sugar: 17g

PEAR GINGER COMPOTE WITH CRUNCHY QUINOA

PREPARATION TIME: 10 min.

COOKING TIME: 20 min.

SERVINGS: 4

M.OF COOKING: Simmering

INGREDIENTS:

- 4 medium pears, peeled and diced
- 2 Tbls grated fresh ginger
- ¼ C. water
- 2 Tbls honey
- ½ tsp ground cinnamon
- ¼ C. cooked quinoa
- 2 Tbls pumpkin seeds

DIRECTIONS:

- In a saucepan, combine pears, fresh ginger, water, honey, and ground cinnamon
- Simmer over medium heat until pears are soft and the liquid thickens, about 20 min.
- Serve warm topped with cooked quinoa and pumpkin seeds

TIPS:

- Can be served over Greek yogurt or cottage cheese for added protein
- Compote can be stored in the refrigerator and used as a topping for pancakes or waffles

N.V. : Calories: 150, Fat: 2g, Carbs: 32g, Protein: 2g, Sugar: 20g

KIWI LIME POPSICLES

PREPARATION TIME: 10 min.

COOKING TIME: none

SERVINGS: 6

M.OF COOKING: Freezing

INGREDIENTS:

- 4 ripe kiwis, peeled and sliced
- Juice of 2 limes
- Zest of 1 lime
- 2 Tbls honey

- ½ C. water
- 6 popsicle sticks

DIRECTIONS:

- In a blender, puree kiwis, lime juice, lime zest, honey, and water until smooth
- Pour the mixture into popsicle molds
- Insert popsicle sticks and freeze until solid, at least 4 hr.

TIPS:

- To remove popsicles easily, run the mold under warm water for a few seconds
- Feel free to add slices of kiwi into the molds for added texture and visual appeal

N.V. : Calories: 60, Fat: 0.5g, Carbs: 14g, Protein: 1g, Sugar: 11g

7.2 HEALTHY BAKES AND PASTRIES

Stepping into the fragrant world of freshly baked goods doesn't mean having to say farewell to your whole food principles. In this delightful section, we'll whisk together the magic of healthy bakes and pastries, proving that indulgence can coexist with nourishment. From the first flaky layers of a butter-less croissant to the last crumb of a vegan muffin, you're about to redefine dessert.

As we sift through these recipes, you'll discover how whole grains, natural sweeteners, and unprocessed oils can transform the art of baking. Each recipe has been crafted with the intention to please not just the palate but also to serve the body. Imagine biting into a warm, spiced banana bread that's not only soul-satisfying but also kind to your well-being—it's these moments of joy that we're going to create together. Let's celebrate the sweet side of health with each scrumptious bite.

SPELT AND ZUCCHINI MUFFINS

PREPARATION TIME: 15 min.

COOKING TIME: 20 min.

SERVINGS: 12

M.OF COOKING: Baking

INGREDIENTS:

- 2 C. spelt flour
- 1 Tbls baking powder
- ½ tsp sea salt
- 1 tsp ground cinnamon
- ¼ C. coconut oil, melted
- ½ C. raw honey
- 1 large egg, beaten
- ¾ C. almond milk
- 1 tsp vanilla extract
- 1½ C. grated zucchini
- ½ C. walnuts, chopped

DIRECTIONS:

- Preheat oven to 350°F (175°C)
- In a large bowl, whisk together spelt flour, baking powder, salt, and cinnamon
- In another bowl, combine melted coconut oil, honey, egg, almond milk, and vanilla extract
- Add wet ingredients to dry, stirring until just combined

- Fold in grated zucchini and walnuts
- Spoon batter into greased muffin tins and bake until a toothpick comes out clean

TIPS:
- Opt for raw, unfiltered honey for additional nutrients
- Squeeze excess moisture from zucchini to prevent soggy muffins
- Muffins can be frozen for grab-and-go breakfasts

N.V. : Calories: 180, Fat: 8g, Carbs: 24g, Protein: 4g, Sugar: 10g

BLACK BEAN BROWNIE BITES

PREPARATION TIME: 10 min.

COOKING TIME: 25 min.

SERVINGS: 16

M. OF COOKING: Baking

INGREDIENTS:
- 1½ C. black beans, drained and rinsed
- 2 large eggs
- 1/3 C. melted coconut oil
- 1/4 C. cocoa powder, unsweetened
- 2/3 C. coconut sugar
- 1 tsp vanilla extract
- ½ tsp baking powder
- ¼ tsp sea salt
- ½ C. dark chocolate chips

DIRECTIONS:
- Preheat oven to 350°F (175°C)
- Blend black beans in a food processor until smooth
- Add eggs, coconut oil, cocoa powder, coconut sugar, vanilla, baking powder, and sea salt to the processor and blend until combined
- Stir in chocolate chips
- Pour the batter into greased mini muffin tins

- Bake until the tops are firm and edges slightly crispy

TIPS:
- Include a scoop of protein powder for an added nutritional boost
- Use high-quality, fair-trade cocoa powder for richer flavor
- Store in an airtight container to maintain freshness

N.V. : Calories: 140, Fat: 7g, Carbs: 17g, Protein: 3g, Sugar: 8g

CHAI SPICED PEAR SCONES

PREPARATION TIME: 20 min.

COOKING TIME: 15 min.

SERVINGS: 8

M. OF COOKING: Baking

INGREDIENTS:
- 2 C. whole wheat pastry flour
- 1 Tbls baking powder
- 1 Tbls chai spice mix
- 1/4 C. coconut oil, solid
- 1/3 C. almond milk
- 1 large egg
- 1/4 C. maple syrup
- 1 ripe pear, cored and diced
- 1 tsp vanilla extract

DIRECTIONS:
- Preheat oven to 425°F (220°C)
- In a bowl, mix together flour, baking powder, and chai spice
- Cut in solid coconut oil until mixture resembles coarse crumbs
- Whisk together almond milk, egg, maple syrup, and vanilla extract in a separate bowl
- Add wet ingredients to dry, mix until just combined
- Gently fold in diced pear
- Form into a round, cut into wedges
- Bake until golden brown

TIPS:

- Rub coconut oil into the flour with your fingertips for a flakier texture
- Serve with a dollop of coconut cream
- Spices are customizable according to taste preferences

N.V. : Calories: 210, Fat: 8g, Carbs: 32g, Protein: 4g, Sugar: 10g

PUMPKIN SEED BRITTLE

PREPARATION TIME: 10 min.

COOKING TIME: 15 min.

SERVINGS: 10

M.OF COOKING: Candy Making

INGREDIENTS:

- 1 C. pumpkin seeds, raw and shelled
- ½ C. coconut sugar
- ¼ C. water
- 1 Tbls coconut oil
- 1 tsp vanilla extract
- ¼ tsp sea salt
- ⅛ tsp baking soda

DIRECTIONS:

- In a heavy-bottomed saucepan, combine coconut sugar, water, and coconut oil, cook over medium heat until sugar dissolves
- Stir in pumpkin seeds and cook until mixture becomes golden brown
- Remove from heat, quickly stir in vanilla extract, baking soda, and sea salt
- Pour mixture onto a baking sheet lined with parchment paper and spread into a thin layer
- Let cool until hardened, then break into pieces

TIPS:

- Grease your spatula with extra coconut oil to prevent sticking
- Use a candy thermometer to ensure the proper temperature

- Try sprinkling with a touch of ground cinnamon for extra flavor

N.V. : Calories: 130, Fat: 8g, Carbs: 12g, Protein: 3g, Sugar: 8g

LEMON LAVENDER TEA CAKES

PREPARATION TIME: 15 min.

COOKING TIME: 22 min.

SERVINGS: 12

M.OF COOKING: Baking

INGREDIENTS:

- 1½ C. almond flour
- ½ C. coconut flour
- 1 tsp baking powder
- ¼ tsp sea salt
- ½ C. ghee, softened
- ¾ C. coconut sugar
- 4 eggs
- 1 Tbls dried lavender flowers, finely ground
- 2 Tbls lemon zest
- ¼ C. lemon juice
- 1 tsp vanilla extract

DIRECTIONS:

- Preheat oven to 350°F (175°C)
- Whisk together almond flour, coconut flour, baking powder, and salt
- In another bowl, cream ghee and coconut sugar until light and fluffy
- Beat in eggs one at a time
- Stir in ground lavender, lemon zest, lemon juice, and vanilla extract
- Gradually add dry ingredients to wet until well combined
- Pour batter into greased and floured mini bundt or loaf pans
- Bake until a toothpick inserted comes out clean

TIPS:

- Be sure to use culinary-grade lavender

- If desired, drizzle with a simple glaze made from lemon juice and coconut sugar
- All ingredients should be at room temperature to ensure even baking

N.V. : Calories: 220, Fat: 16g, Carbs: 18g, Protein: 6g, Sugar: 9g

MATCHA GREEN TEA COOKIES

PREPARATION TIME: 12 min.

COOKING TIME: 10 min.

SERVINGS: 24

M.OF COOKING: Baking

INGREDIENTS:

- 2 C. almond flour
- 1 Tbls matcha green tea powder
- ¼ tsp sea salt
- ¼ tsp baking soda
- ⅓ C. coconut oil, melted
- ½ C. maple syrup
- 1 tsp vanilla extract

DIRECTIONS:

- Preheat oven to 350°F (175°C)
- Whisk together almond flour, matcha powder, sea salt, and baking soda
- In a separate bowl, mix melted coconut oil, maple syrup, and vanilla extract
- Add wet ingredients to dry and stir until combined
- Drop tablespoons of the dough onto a parchment-lined baking sheet
- Bake until edges are just turning golden

TIPS:

- Ensure matcha powder is fully sifted to avoid clumps
- Cookies will retain a soft center due to almond flour
- Rest the dough for 10 minutes before baking to deepen flavors

N.V. : Calories: 100, Fat: 8g, Carbs: 6g, Protein: 2g, Sugar: 4g

FESTIVE FRUIT AND NUT TART

PREPARATION TIME: 30 min.

COOKING TIME: 40 min.

SERVINGS: 8

M.OF COOKING: Baking

INGREDIENTS:

- 1 C. almond flour
- 1 C. oat flour
- ¼ C. coconut oil, chilled
- 2 Tbls maple syrup
- 1 tsp almond extract
- ½ tsp sea salt
- Filling: 1 C. mixed dried fruits, chopped
- ¾ C. chopped nuts of choice
- ¼ C. orange juice
- Zest of 1 orange
- ½ tsp ground cinnamon
- ¼ tsp ground nutmeg
- 1 Tbls arrowroot powder

DIRECTIONS:

- Preheat oven to 375°F (190°C)
- Combine almond flour, oat flour, and sea salt in a bowl
- Cut in chilled coconut oil until mixture resembles coarse crumbs
- Stir in maple syrup and almond extract until dough forms
- Press dough into a tart pan and pre-bake for 10 minutes
- For filling, combine dried fruits, nuts, orange juice, zest, cinnamon, and nutmeg in a saucepan and cook over medium heat until fruits are plump
- Stir in arrowroot powder to thicken
- Pour filling into pre-baked crust and bake until golden

TIPS:

- Soak dried fruits in warm orange juice for 10 minutes prior to cooking for enhanced flavor

- Decorate with sliced almonds or fresh fruit for a festive look

7.3 NO-ADDED-SUGAR DESSERTS

Conquering the sweet tooth without surrendering to the siren call of sugar is an art—and in this chapter, we elevate that art to new heights. Our no-added-sugar desserts are crafted to charm your taste buds while honoring your body's needs, employing the natural sweetness of fruits and the richness of whole ingredients to do so. Imagine indulging in a creamy dessert, with every spoonful as guilt-free as it is delectable. Whether it's a velvety avocado chocolate mousse or baked apples with a pinch of cinnamon warmth, these treats prove that nature is the most skilled confectioner. We've stripped away the excess, leaving only pure, unadulterated joy that will have your family clamoring for seconds. These scrumptious finales to your meal will redefine how you view dessert, turning the final course into a celebration of natural flavors that truly nourish.

CHIA & BERRY GELATO

PREPARATION TIME: 15 min

COOKING TIME: none

SERVINGS: 4

M.OF COOKING: No Cooking

INGREDIENTS:

- 2 C. coconut milk
- 1 C. mixed berries, fresh or frozen
- 3 Tbls chia seeds
- ½ tsp vanilla extract
- Mint leaves for garnish

DIRECTIONS:

- Blend coconut milk, mixed berries, and vanilla extract until smooth

- Stir in chia seeds and let the mixture rest for 10 minutes until it begins to thicken

- Pour into an airtight container and freeze until set, stirring occasionally

TIPS:

- Serve with a dollop of whipped coconut cream for added indulgence

N.V. : Calories: 310, Fat: 20g, Carbs: 28g, Protein: 6g, Sugar: 12g

- Garnish with fresh mint leaves for added color and a refreshing taste

- Use a combination of blueberries, raspberries, and strawberries for a vibrant mix

- If using frozen berries, thaw slightly before blending

N.V. : Calories: 200, Fat: 15g, Carbs: 15g, Protein: 3g, Sugar: 0g

AVOCADO CHOCOLATE MOUSSE

PREPARATION TIME: 10 min

COOKING TIME: none

SERVINGS: 2

M.OF COOKING: No Cooking

INGREDIENTS:

- 1 ripe avocado, pitted and scooped
- 2 Tbls raw cacao powder
- 2 Tbls almond milk
- 1 tsp pure vanilla extract
- 1 tsp cinnamon

- Pinch of sea salt

DIRECTIONS:

- Puree avocado, cacao powder, almond milk, vanilla extract, cinnamon, and sea salt in a blender until smooth
- Spoon into serving dishes and chill in the refrigerator until ready to serve

TIPS:

- Serve with a sprinkle of cacao nibs for a crunchy texture
- For a more pronounced flavor, add a splash of espresso or coffee extract
- Sweeten with a dab of raw honey or pure maple syrup if desired, but remember the goal is to keep sugars to an absolute minimum

N.V. : Calories: 220, Fat: 17g, Carbs: 19g, Protein: 4g, Sugar: 0g

ROASTED CINNAMON PEARS

PREPARATION TIME: 5 min
COOKING TIME: 25 min
SERVINGS: 4
M.OF COOKING: Baking
INGREDIENTS:

- 4 ripe pears, halved and cored
- 1 tsp ground cinnamon
- ½ tsp ground nutmeg
- 2 tsp coconut oil
- A few drops of almond extract

DIRECTIONS:

- Preheat oven to 350°F (175°C)
- Place pear halves on a baking sheet and drizzle with coconut oil, almond extract, and sprinkle with cinnamon and nutmeg
- Roast in the oven until tender and slightly caramelized

TIPS:

- Serve warm, perhaps with a dollop of coconut cream
- Pair with a cup of herbal tea for a comforting dessert experience
- Select pears that are just ripe enough to maintain shape when roasted

N.V. : Calories: 110, Fat: 3g, Carbs: 22g, Protein: 1g, Sugar: 15g

ALMOND LEMON BITES

PREPARATION TIME: 20 min
COOKING TIME: none
SERVINGS: 10
M.OF COOKING: No Cooking
INGREDIENTS:

- 1½ C. almond flour
- Zest of 2 lemons
- ¼ C. unsweetened coconut flakes
- 1 Tbls lemon juice
- 1 tsp vanilla extract
- 3 Tbls coconut oil
- A pinch of Himalayan pink salt

DIRECTIONS:

- Combine all ingredients in a food processor until mixture sticks together
- Roll into small bite-sized balls and chill in the refrigerator

TIPS:

- Roll the bites in extra coconut flakes or lemon zest for more flavor and texture
- Can be stored in an airtight container in the refrigerator for up to one week

N.V. : Calories: 100, Fat: 9g, Carbs: 3g, Protein: 2g, Sugar: 1g

COCONUT FLOUR FIG BARS

PREPARATION TIME: 20 min
COOKING TIME: 30 min
SERVINGS: 12
M.OF COOKING: Baking
INGREDIENTS:

- ⅓ C. coconut flour
- 6 dried figs, soaked and pureed

- ¼ C. apple sauce, unsweetened
- 2 Tbls ground flax seeds
- ½ C. water
- 1 Tbls cinnamon
- A pinch of cardamom
- ½ tsp baking soda

DIRECTIONS:

- Preheat oven to 350°F (175°C)
- Mix ground flax seeds with water, set aside to form flax egg
- Combine coconut flour, cinnamon, cardamom, and baking soda
- Mix in flax egg, fig puree, and apple sauce until well combined
- Press dough into a lined baking pan
- Bake until edges are golden brown

TIPS:

- Cut into bars while still warm for easier slicing
- Wrap individual bars for on-the-go snacks
- Can be frozen for longer shelf life

N.V. : Calories: 90, Fat: 1g, Carbs: 17g, Protein: 2g, Sugar: 8g

FROZEN BANANA CREAM POPS

PREPARATION TIME: 15 min

COOKING TIME: 4 hr

SERVINGS: 6

M.OF COOKING: Freezing

INGREDIENTS:

- 3 ripe bananas
- 1 C. Greek yogurt, unsweetened
- 2 tsp pure vanilla extract
- ¼ tsp ground cinnamon
- ¼ C. crushed walnuts
- 6 popsicle sticks

DIRECTIONS:

- Puree bananas, Greek yogurt, vanilla extract, and cinnamon in a blender until smooth

- Stir in crushed walnuts
- Pour the mixture into popsicle molds and insert popsicle sticks
- Freeze until firm

TIPS:

- Dip the pops in dark chocolate and freeze again for a delightful shell
- To remove pops from molds, run under warm water for a few seconds
- Experiment with different nuts or seeds to find your favorite crunchy inclusion

N.V. : Calories: 120, Fat: 3g, Carbs: 20g, Protein: 5g, Sugar: 10g

SPICED PEAR SORBET

PREPARATION TIME: 15 min

COOKING TIME: 2 hr

SERVINGS: 4

M.OF COOKING: Freezing

INGREDIENTS:

- 4 C. pears, ripe and diced
- Juice of 1 lemon
- ½ tsp ground ginger
- ¼ tsp ground cloves
- 1 tsp vanilla extract
- ½ C. water
- 1 Tbls fresh mint, finely chopped

DIRECTIONS:

- Blend pears, lemon juice, ginger, cloves, vanilla extract, and water until smooth
- Pour the mixture into a shallow tray and freeze until semi-solid
- Once partially frozen, scrape with a fork and mix in fresh mint
- Return to the freezer until completely frozen

TIPS:

- Serve scooped into bowls or glasses
- Garnish with a sprig of mint or a dusting of ground cinnamon for a spiced kick

• Pears can be roasted prior to blending for a deeper flavor

N.V. : Calories: 100, Fat: 0g, Carbs: 26g, Protein: 1g, Sugar: 17g

CHAPTER 8: BEVERAGES AND SMOOTHIES

8.1 NUTRIENT-PACKED GREEN SMOOTHIES

Welcome to the verdant world of green smoothies—a sanctuary for those yearning to infuse their days with a burst of vitality. Imagine sipping on a concoction where every drop pulsates with nutrients, weaving the raw life-force of leafy greens with the succulent sweetness of fruits. In this subchapter, we herald a celebration of flavors as much as a symphony of health. Uniting kale's robust whispers with the tender murmur of spinach, and a hint of fresh herbs for a zesty note, each smoothie stands as an ode to nature's brilliance.

Green smoothies are the unsung heroes in our quest for wellness. With a whirl of the blender, we create potions that deliver vitality, aid digestion, and brighten our complexions—truly a glass of goodness to begin our day with a promise of well-being. Let us embark on this journey with joy, knowing that with each blend, we are one step closer to a thriving, nourished life.

KALEIDOSCOPE GREEN ESSENCE

Kaleidosope Essence

PREPARATION TIME: 5 min
COOKING TIME: none
SERVINGS: 2
M.OF COOKING: Blending
INGREDIENTS:
- 1 large hand-torn bunch of kale
- 1 peeled and cored tart green apple
- ½ ripe avocado
- 1 C. fresh pineapple chunks
- 1 Tbls chia seeds
- 2 C. cold coconut water
- 1 tsp freshly grated ginger
- 1 Tbls fresh lemon juice

DIRECTIONS:
- Combine all ingredients in a high-speed blender
- Blend on high until smooth and creamy
- Pour into glasses and serve immediately

TIPS:
- Add a handful of fresh spinach for an extra boost of greens
- Use frozen pineapple for a colder, thicker smoothie

N.V. : Calories: 224, Fat: 6g, Carbs: 42g, Protein: 4g, Sugar: 25g

MINTY PEA PROTEIN POTION

PREPARATION TIME: 5 min
COOKING TIME: none
SERVINGS: 1
M.OF COOKING: Blending

INGREDIENTS:

- 1 C. frozen peas
- 1 ripe banana
- ¼ C. packed fresh mint leaves
- 1 Tbls hemp hearts
- 1 C. cold water
- 1 scoop plant-based vanilla protein powder
- Juice of half a lime
- 1 tsp raw honey

DIRECTIONS:

- Puree all ingredients in a blender until fully combined and velvety
- Taste and adjust sweetness if needed
- Enjoy immediately for the most vibrant flavor

TIPS:

- Experiment with adding cucumber for extra hydration
- Drizzle with a teaspoon of flaxseed oil for an omega-3 boost

N.V. : Calories: 330, Fat: 4g, Carbs: 48g, Protein: 27g, Sugar: 22g

SPIRULINA SUNRISE ELIXIR

PREPARATION TIME: 5 min
COOKING TIME: none
SERVINGS: 1
M.OF COOKING: Blending
INGREDIENTS:

- 1 C. organic baby spinach
- ½ C. frozen mango chunks
- ½ C. frozen peach slices
- 1 Tbls spirulina powder
- 1 Tbls golden flaxseed meal
- 1½ C. unsweetened almond milk
- 1 Tbls maple syrup
- 1 tsp vanilla extract

DIRECTIONS:

- Start by blending the spinach and almond milk until smooth
- Add the remaining ingredients to the mixture and blend until you achieve a rich, smooth consistency
- Pour into a chilled glass and savor

TIPS:

- Swap the maple syrup for a few drops of stevia if you prefer a lower glycemic index
- Garnish with a few slices of peach to beautify your beverage

N.V. : Calories: 215, Fat: 3g, Carbs: 39g, Protein: 8g, Sugar: 27g

GREEN TEA DETOXIFIER

PREPARATION TIME: 7 min
COOKING TIME: none
SERVINGS: 2
M.OF COOKING: Blending
INGREDIENTS:

- 1 C. brewed and chilled green tea
- 1 C. tightly packed swiss chard leaves
- 1 small peeled cucumber
- ½ C. fresh parsley leaves
- 1 small green apple, quartered
- 1 Tbls raw honey
- Juice of 1 lemon

DIRECTIONS:

- Blend the swiss chard, cucumber, parsley, and green tea until smooth
- Add the apple, honey, lemon juice, and blend again until smooth
- Serve chilled for a refreshing detox experience

TIPS:

- Feel free to add a knob of turmeric or ginger for their anti-inflammatory properties
- If you desire more sweetness, throw in a couple of ripe kiwi fruits

N.V. : Calories: 98, Fat: 0.5g, Carbs: 25g, Protein: 2g, Sugar: 18g

BERRY BASIL VITALITY SHAKE

PREPARATION TIME: 6 min

COOKING TIME: none

SERVINGS: 2

M. OF COOKING: Blending

INGREDIENTS:

- 1 C. fresh spinach leaves
- ½ C. frozen blueberries
- ½ C. frozen raspberries
- 4 fresh basil leaves
- 1 Tbls almond butter
- 1½ C. oat milk
- 1 Tbls goji berries
- 1 Tbls agave nectar

DIRECTIONS:

- Blend spinach, berries, basil, and oat milk until smooth
- Add almond butter, goji berries, agave nectar and blend once more until shake like in texture
- Serve immediately to enjoy the freshness

TIPS:

- Try adding a few slices of avocado for a creamier texture
- Sprinkle a dash of cinnamon on top for a warming note

N.V. : Calories: 240, Fat: 8g, Carbs: 38g, Protein: 5g, Sugar: 20g

AVOCADO LIME REFRESHER

PREPARATION TIME: 4 min

COOKING TIME: none

SERVINGS: 1

M. OF COOKING: Blending

INGREDIENTS:

- 1 fully ripened avocado
- 1½ C. fresh baby kale leaves
- 1 C. cold water
- Juice of 2 limes
- 1 Tbls raw honey
- 1 Tbls chia seeds
- Ice cubes as needed
- 1 tsp matcha powder

DIRECTIONS:

- Blend avocado, kale, water, lime juice, and matcha powder until smooth
- Add honey, chia seeds, and ice cubes and blend again until you reach a frosty consistency
- Indulge in this energizing smoothie bowl-style or as a drink

TIPS:

- If you crave a bit more sweetness, drizzle in a touch more honey
- Enhance the matcha flavor by sprinkling a pinch of matcha powder on top before serving

N.V. : Calories: 345, Fat: 21g, Carbs: 39g, Protein: 6g, Sugar: 18g

ZESTY GINGER COLLARD COOLER

PREPARATION TIME: 6 min

COOKING TIME: none

SERVINGS: 2

M. OF COOKING: Blending

INGREDIENTS:

- 2 C. stripped and chopped collard greens
- 1 C. diced honeydew melon
- ½ C. chopped cucumber
- 1 peeled and sliced kiwi
- 2 Tbls fresh ginger root, grated
- 1½ C. green tea, chilled
- Juice of 1 orange

DIRECTIONS:

- Combine collard greens, cucumber, kiwi, ginger, and half the green tea in your blender and mix until smooth

- Add the remaining tea, honeydew melon, and orange juice; blend again
- Enjoy this zesty cooler on a hot day or whenever you need a refreshing nutrient kick

TIPS:

- Throw in a few leaves of fresh mint for an invigorating twist
- A scoop of collagen peptides can add an extra layer of skin-loving nutrients

N.V. : Calories: 110, Fat: 1g, Carbs: 27g, Protein: 4g, Sugar: 14g

8.2 HERBAL TEAS AND INFUSIONS

Embracing the garden's quiet whisper and the wisdom of the leaves, herbal teas and infusions are the serene symphony to your day's bustling overture. Think of these beverages as liquid tranquility—a gentle nudge towards relaxation, a nod to the time-honored traditions of holistic well-being. Imagine yourself cradling a warm mug, steam rising like a spirit, whilst every sip beckons a deeper communion with nature's own apothecary. In this sub-chapter, we'll explore an array of herbal wonders, from the vibrant zest of lemon balm to the soothing embrace of chamomile. Each infusion, a seamless tapestry of flavors and benefits, woven with care, just as nature intended. Unravel with me the delicate art of selecting, blending, and brewing these herbal elixirs, as we pour out the old myths and steep ourselves into the heart of what it means to truly drink in the goodness of the earth.

CALMING CHAMOMILE AND LAVENDER BLEND

PREPARATION TIME: 5 min

COOKING TIME: 10 min

SERVINGS: 2

M.OF COOKING: Steeping

INGREDIENTS:

- 1 Tbls dried chamomile flowers
- 1 tsp dried lavender buds
- 2 C. boiling water
- Honey or lemon to taste

DIRECTIONS:

- Place chamomile and lavender in a teapot or heat-proof jar
- Pour boiling water over the herbs and cover
- Steep for 10 min.
- Strain into cups and add honey or lemon if desired

TIPS:

- Honey enhances the natural sweetness of the tea
- For a stronger infusion, allow to steep for an additional 5 min

N.V. : Calories: 2, Fat: 0g, Carbs: 0.5g, Protein: 0g, Sugar: 0g

MINTY NETTLE DETOX INFUSION

PREPARATION TIME: 5 min

COOKING TIME: 15 min

SERVINGS: 4

M.OF COOKING: Steeping

INGREDIENTS:

- 1/4 C. fresh nettle leaves
- 1/4 C. fresh mint leaves
- 4 C. boiling water

- Lemon slices for garnish

DIRECTIONS:

- Rinse nettle and mint leaves thoroughly
- Place herbs in a large teapot
- Add boiling water and allow to steep covered for 15 min.
- Strain and serve with a slice of lemon

TIPS:

- Using fresh leaves can create a more potent infusion
- Can be served chilled for a refreshing summer drink
- Always handle nettle with gloves to avoid stinging

N.V. : Calories: 0, Fat: 0g, Carbs: 0g, Protein: 0g, Sugar: 0g

ROSEHIP AND HIBISCUS HEART TONIC

PREPARATION TIME: 7 min

COOKING TIME: 5 min

SERVINGS: 2

M.OF COOKING: Simmering

INGREDIENTS:

- 2 Tbls dried rosehips
- 1 Tbls dried hibiscus petals
- 2.5 C. water
- 1 tsp raw honey

DIRECTIONS:

- Bring water to a light simmer
- Add rosehips and hibiscus
- Simmer for 5 min.
- Remove from heat and let steep for an additional 2 min.
- Strain into cups and sweeten with honey if desired

TIPS:

- A rich source of Vitamin C, this tonic is wonderful for skin health
- A pinch of cinnamon can add a warming touch

- The longer you steep, the more robust the flavor

N.V. : Calories: 9, Fat: 0g, Carbs: 2g, Protein: 0g, Sugar: 1.5g

SPICED TURMERIC AND GINGER TEA

PREPARATION TIME: 10 min

COOKING TIME: 20 min

SERVINGS: 3

M.OF COOKING: Simmering

INGREDIENTS:

- 1 Tbls turmeric root, grated
- 1 Tbls ginger root, grated
- 3 C. water
- 1/2 tsp black pepper
- 1 Tbls lemon juice
- 1 Tbls honey

DIRECTIONS:

- Combine water, turmeric, and ginger in a pot and bring to a simmer
- Add black pepper (to enhance turmeric absorption)
- Simmer for 20 min.
- Remove from heat, add lemon juice and honey
- Strain and serve

TIPS:

- Drink it in the evening for an anti-inflammatory boost
- The turmeric stain can be removed with baking soda
- Adjust honey to suit your sweetness level

N.V. : Calories: 24, Fat: 0g, Carbs: 6g, Protein: 0g, Sugar: 6g

DANDELION ROOT DIGESTIVE AID

PREPARATION TIME: 5 min

COOKING TIME: 30 min

SERVINGS: 4

M.OF COOKING: Decoction

INGREDIENTS:

- 1/4 C. dandelion root, chopped
- 4 C. water

DIRECTIONS:

- In a saucepan, cover dandelion root with water
- Bring to a boil then reduce heat to simmer for 30 min.
- Strain the decoction into mugs

TIPS:

- Dandelion root is known for supporting liver health
- Serve with a slice of orange to counter the bitterness
- Can be enjoyed before meals to aid digestion

N.V.: Calories: 0, Fat: 0g, Carbs: 0g, Protein: 0g, Sugar: 0g

ELDERFLOWER IMMUNE BOOSTING ELIXIR

PREPARATION TIME: 8 min

COOKING TIME: none

SERVINGS: 1

M.OF COOKING: Steeping

INGREDIENTS:

- 2 Tbls dried elderflowers
- 1 C. hot water
- 1 tsp lemon zest
- Raw honey to taste

DIRECTIONS:

- Place elderflowers and lemon zest in a cup
- Cover with hot water
- Cover and let steep for 8 min.
- Strain and sweeten with honey as desired

TIPS:

- Elderflower is traditionally used to fortify the immune system
- Can be paired with a pinch of cinnamon for added benefits
- Always ensure flowers are correctly identified as elderflowers

N.V.: Calories: 6, Fat: 0g, Carbs: 1.5g, Protein: 0g, Sugar: 1.5g

SOOTHING LEMON BALM AND SAGE TEA

PREPARATION TIME: 5 min

COOKING TIME: 10 min

SERVINGS: 2

M.OF COOKING: Steeping

INGREDIENTS:

- 1 Tbls dried lemon balm
- 1 tsp dried sage leaves
- 2 C. boiling water

DIRECTIONS:

- Put lemon balm and sage into a tea infuser or directly into a teapot
- Pour boiling water over the herbs
- Let them steep for 10 min
- Strain and serve

TIPS:

- Lemon balm aids in reducing stress while sage has memory-enhancing properties
- Adding a slice of fresh ginger can enhance the digestive benefits
- May be sweetened with a small spoonful of honey or enjoyed on its own

N.V.: Calories: 2, Fat: 0g, Carbs: 0.5g, Protein: 0g, Sugar: 0g

8.3 HOMEMADE NUT MILKS AND NATURAL JUICES

Embark on a journey to revitalize your hydration habits with the hidden gems of homemade nut milks and natural juices. These handcrafted beverages are more than thirst quenchers—they're a revolution in your glass, a pure blend of nutrition and taste without the additives that often accompany store-bought alternatives. Imagine sipping on almond milk, tailor-made to your preference, or a vibrant, freshly-pressed juice that captures the essence of sun-ripened fruits—it's nature's indulgence at your fingertips.

In this section, we'll explore the simple artistry behind creating these wholesome drinks in your own kitchen. You'll learn how to unlock the full potential of nuts and seeds, transforming them into milks that are both creamy and nourishing. We'll also guide you in concocting juices that burst with life, harnessing the raw vitality of fruits and vegetables. These sips of goodness are not only a boon for your body but also a canvas for your culinary creativity, blending well-being with the sheer pleasure of taste.

CLASSIC ALMOND MILK

PREPARATION TIME: 10 min

COOKING TIME: none

SERVINGS: 4 cups

M. OF COOKING: No Cooking

INGREDIENTS:
- 1 C. raw almonds, soaked overnight
- 4 C. filtered water
- 1 tsp vanilla extract (optional)
- 2 Tbls maple syrup or honey (optional)
- Pinch of sea salt

DIRECTIONS:
- Drain and rinse the almonds
- Blend almonds with filtered water until smooth
- Strain mixture using a nut milk bag or cheesecloth
- Return the liquid to the blender, add vanilla extract, sweetener, and sea salt, then blend again

TIPS:
- Soak almonds for up to 48 hours for a creamier milk
- Add soaked dates or banana for natural sweetness
- Use leftover almond pulp for baking or as a facial scrub

N.V. : Calories: 30, Fat: 2g, Carbs: 1g, Protein: 1g, Sugar: 0.7g

SPICED CASHEW MILK

PREPARATION TIME: 15 min

COOKING TIME: none

SERVINGS: 4 cups

M. OF COOKING: No Cooking

INGREDIENTS:
- 1 C. raw cashews, soaked 4 hr.
- 4 C. warm water
- 1 tsp ground cinnamon
- ½ tsp ground nutmeg
- 1 tsp vanilla extract
- 2 Tbls agave syrup

DIRECTIONS:
- Drain and rinse soaked cashews

- Blend cashews with warm water on high speed until creamy
- Incorporate cinnamon, nutmeg, vanilla extract, and agave syrup
- Strain through a fine-mesh sieve or nut milk bag

TIPS:

- Add a pinch of cardamom for an exotic twist
- Nut milk can be stored for up to 4 days in the fridge
- Use cashew milk as a creamer in coffee or tea for added richness

N.V. : Calories: 40, Fat: 3g, Carbs: 2g, Protein: 1.5g, Sugar: 1.2g

GOLDEN MACADAMIA MILK

PREPARATION TIME: 10 min

COOKING TIME: none

SERVINGS: 4 cups

M.OF COOKING: No Cooking

INGREDIENTS:

- 1 C. raw macadamia nuts, soaked 2 hr.
- 4 C. water
- 1 Tbls honey
- ½ tsp turmeric powder
- ¼ tsp ginger powder
- A dash of black pepper

DIRECTIONS:

- Drain and rinse macadamia nuts
- Blend nuts with water until smooth
- Add honey, turmeric, ginger, and black pepper to the blender
- Blend until combined
- Strain through a fine-mesh strainer or nut milk bag

TIPS:

- Turmeric enhances anti-inflammatory benefits

- Sweeten with a date for a more natural option
- Macadamia milk is particularly rich and indulgent for desserts

N.V. : Calories: 50, Fat: 5g, Carbs: 1g, Protein: 0.5g, Sugar: 1g

SESAME SEED MILK

PREPARATION TIME: 8 min

COOKING TIME: none

SERVINGS: 3 cups

M.OF COOKING: No Cooking

INGREDIENTS:

- 1 C. white sesame seeds, soaked 8 hr.
- 3 C. water
- 1 tsp vanilla extract
- 1 Tbls agave nectar
- Pinch of salt

DIRECTIONS:

- Drain and rinse sesame seeds
- Blend seeds with water until well combined
- Include vanilla extract, agave nectar, and salt
- Strain through a nut milk bag or cheesecloth
- Serve chilled or use in cereal

TIPS:

- Sesame seeds are high in calcium and perfect for those avoiding nuts
- Use sesame milk in savory dishes for an added nutty flavor
- Combine with dates or figs for a sweeter profile

N.V. : Calories: 60, Fat: 4.5g, Carbs: 2g, Protein: 2g, Sugar: 0.5g

HEMP HEART HORCHATA

PREPARATION TIME: 10 min

COOKING TIME: none

SERVINGS: 6 cups

M.OF COOKING: No Cooking

INGREDIENTS:

- 1 C. hemp hearts
- 6 C. filtered water
- 1 cinnamon stick
- 1 tsp vanilla extract
- ¼ C. maple syrup
- Ground cinnamon for garnish

DIRECTIONS:

- Blend hemp hearts and filtered water until smooth
- Pour mixture over a cinnamon stick in a large pitcher and refrigerate for at least 2 hrs
- Stir in vanilla extract and maple syrup
- Serve over ice with a sprinkle of ground cinnamon

TIPS:

- Hemp hearts add a boost of omega fatty acids to this traditional drink
- Sweeten with dried fruits for variation
- Hemp horchata can be a protein-packed snack or a refreshing post-workout drink

N.V. : Calories: 70, Fat: 5g, Carbs: 4g, Protein: 3g, Sugar: 3g

PECAN PIE MILK

PREPARATION TIME: 12 min

COOKING TIME: none

SERVINGS: 4 cups

M.OF COOKING: No Cooking

INGREDIENTS:

- 1 C. raw pecans, soaked overnight
- 4 C. water
- 1 Tbls pure maple syrup
- 2 tsp vanilla extract
- 1 tsp ground cinnamon
- A pinch of ground clove
- A pinch of sea salt

DIRECTIONS:

- Drain and rinse pecans
- Blend pecans and water until smooth
- Introduce maple syrup, vanilla extract, cinnamon, clove, and sea salt
- Strain through a nut milk bag
- Refrigerate and serve chilled

TIPS:

- Indulge in this as a seasonal treat during holidays
- Sweeten naturally with medjool dates
- Pecan milk is a flavorful base for coffee drinks

N.V. : Calories: 80, Fat: 7g, Carbs: 3g, Protein: 1g, Sugar: 2g

COOLING CUCUMBER JUICE

PREPARATION TIME: 5 min

COOKING TIME: none

SERVINGS: 2 cups

M.OF COOKING: No Cooking

INGREDIENTS:

- 2 large cucumbers, peeled and chopped
- Juice of 1 lime
- 2 Tbls fresh mint leaves
- 1 Tbls raw honey
- 2 C. cold water

DIRECTIONS:

- Blend cucumbers, lime juice, mint leaves, and honey with cold water until smooth
- Strain the juice to remove the pulp
- Serve over ice

TIPS:

- Cucumber juice is ideal for hydration and detoxification
- Amplify its cooling effect by adding a slice of ginger
- Serve as a palate cleanser between meals

N.V. : Calories: 38, Fat: 0.2g, Carbs: 9g, Protein: 1g, Sugar: 6g

CHAPTER 9: WHOLE FOOD STAPLES

9.1 HOW TO MAKE NUT AND SEED BUTTERS

Welcome to the enchanting world of homemade nut and seed butters—the heart and soul of a whole food pantry. These delectable spreads are a testament to nature's simplicity, transforming humble ingredients into a symphony of richness and flavor that elevates any meal. Home-crafting your own butters is not just about the unrivaled taste; it's about taking charge of your health with every creamy spoonful. Each jar you create is free from preservatives and packed with nutrients, providing a source of healthy fats and proteins vital to our well-being.

As we journey together through the art of making nut and seed butters, you'll uncover the ease and joy of turning almonds, cashews, sunflower seeds, and more into velvety treasures. Just imagine slathering your morning toast with a spread you've conjured up from scratch or dolloping a rich, homemade almond butter onto a slice of apple. The possibilities are as boundless as your aspirations for healthful, vibrant living. Let's begin this delightful culinary adventure with a blend of excitement and pure, unadulterated wholesomeness.

CLASSIC CREAMY ALMOND BUTTER

PREPARATION TIME: 10 min.

COOKING TIME: 10 min.

SERVINGS: 16

M.OF COOKING: Food Processor

INGREDIENTS:

- 2 C. raw almonds
- ⅛ tsp fine sea salt

DIRECTIONS:

- Roast almonds on baking sheet at 350°F (175°C) for 10 min. until lightly golden and fragrant
- Let cool slightly
- Transfer to food processor and blend until creamy, scraping down sides as necessary

TIPS:

- Add a dash of cinnamon for a warm twist
- Store in glass jar at room temperature to maintain spreadability

N.V. : Calories: 98, Fat: 8.5g, Carbs: 3.5g, Protein: 3.6g, Sugar: 0.7g

SPICED PUMPKIN SEED BUTTER

PREPARATION TIME: 5 min.

COOKING TIME: none

SERVINGS: 12

M.OF COOKING: Food Processor

INGREDIENTS:

- 1.5 C. raw shelled pumpkin seeds
- 1 Tbls pumpkin seed oil
- ¼ tsp ground cinnamon
- ¼ tsp ground nutmeg
- ⅛ tsp ground cloves
- ⅛ tsp fine sea salt

DIRECTIONS:

- Toast pumpkin seeds in a dry skillet over medium heat for 3-4 min. until popped and fragrant
- Transfer to food processor with remaining ingredients and blend until smooth, scraping down sides as needed

TIPS:

- Stir into oatmeal or spread on toast with a drizzle of honey
- Refrigerate in an airtight container to maintain freshness

N.V. : Calories: 150, Fat: 13g, Carbs: 4g, Protein: 7g, Sugar: 0.1g

WALNUT AND FLAXSEED BUTTER

PREPARATION TIME: 8 min.

COOKING TIME: none

SERVINGS: 14

M. OF COOKING: Food Processor

INGREDIENTS:

- 2 C. raw walnuts
- 2 Tbls ground flaxseeds
- 1 Tbls walnut oil
- ⅛ tsp fine sea salt

DIRECTIONS:

- Process walnuts, flaxseeds, and salt in a food processor until finely ground
- With the processor running, drizzle in walnut oil and blend until smooth and spreadable

TIPS:

- A touch of maple syrup can sweeten the mix

- Refrigerate to extend its shelf life and keep the flaxseeds from going rancid

N.V. : Calories: 190, Fat: 17g, Carbs: 4g, Protein: 4g, Sugar: 0.5g

TAHINI (SESAME SEED BUTTER)

PREPARATION TIME: 15 min.

COOKING TIME: none

SERVINGS: 20

M. OF COOKING: Food Processor

INGREDIENTS:

- 3 C. hulled sesame seeds
- 2-4 Tbls neutral oil such as grapeseed or light olive oil
- ⅛ tsp fine sea salt

DIRECTIONS:

- In a skillet, lightly toast sesame seeds over medium heat until golden and fragrant, about 5 min., watch carefully to avoid burning
- Allow seeds to cool
- Blend seeds in food processor, adding oil gradually, until a smooth, pourable consistency is achieved

TIPS:

- Freeze in small portions to add to smoothies or dressings
- Mix with honey for a sweet drizzle on desserts

N.V. : Calories: 100, Fat: 8.8g, Carbs: 3.2g, Protein: 2.8g, Sugar: 0.03g

SUNFLOWER SEED AND CHIA BUTTER

PREPARATION TIME: 10 min.

COOKING TIME: none

SERVINGS: 10

M. OF COOKING: Food Processor

INGREDIENTS:

- 2 C. raw sunflower seeds
- 2 Tbls chia seeds
- 1 Tbls sunflower oil
- ⅛ tsp fine sea salt

DIRECTIONS:

- Process sunflower seeds and chia seeds in food processor until powdery
- While processing, slowly add sunflower oil until the mixture becomes smooth and buttery

TIPS:

- Pair with freshly cut vegetables as a savory dip
- Spread on apple slices for a crunchy snack

N.V. : Calories: 204, Fat: 17.6g, Carbs: 8.4g, Protein: 6.2g, Sugar: 0.7g

CASHEW AND VANILLA BEAN BUTTER

PREPARATION TIME: 12 min.

COOKING TIME: none

SERVINGS: 18

M.OF COOKING: Food Processor

INGREDIENTS:

- 2 C. raw cashews
- 1 Tbls coconut oil
- Seeds from 1 vanilla bean
- ⅛ tsp fine sea salt

DIRECTIONS:

- Blend cashews in a food processor until a fine meal forms
- Slowly incorporate coconut oil and vanilla seeds until smooth and creamy

TIPS:

- A drop of almond extract adds a complex flavor note

- Can be used as a base for vegan creams and desserts

N.V. : Calories: 94, Fat: 7.7g, Carbs: 5.3g, Protein: 2.7g, Sugar: 1g

HERBED MACADAMIA NUT BUTTER

PREPARATION TIME: 15 min.

COOKING TIME: none

SERVINGS: 15

M.OF COOKING: Food Processor

INGREDIENTS:

- 2 C. raw macadamia nuts
- 1 Tbls macadamia oil
- 1 tsp dried rosemary
- 1 tsp dried thyme
- ¼ tsp garlic powder
- ⅛ tsp fine sea salt

DIRECTIONS:

- Blend macadamia nuts until finely ground in a food processor
- Add the herbs, garlic powder, and salt, then drizzle in the oil while blending until the mixture becomes smooth and creamy

TIPS:

- Serve as a spread on a gourmet sandwich or with crackers as an appetizer
- Refrigerate to keep fresh and firm

N.V. : Calories: 204, Fat: 21g, Carbs: 4g, Protein: 2g, Sugar: 1.2g

9.2 PREPARING WHOLE GRAINS AND LEGUMES

Embracing the world of whole grains and legumes is akin to unlocking a treasure chest of nourishment for you and your family. Grains like quinoa, brown rice, and barley, alongside legumes such as lentils, chickpeas, and black beans, are brimming with life-giving nutrients. They are not merely sides or fillers; they are the beating heart of a wholesome meal.

In this cozy corner of our culinary journey, we'll learn the nuances of preparing these gifts from the earth, transforming them from humble raw ingredients into the stars of our plates. It's about more than just boiling and simmering; it's about coaxing out flavors, textures, and health benefits. Releasing the potential of these staples is like weaving a spell in your kitchen—one where every grain and bean bursts with the magic of well-being. Let's step into this dance of preparation with simplicity and joy, knowing that each dish brings us closer to the harmony of whole food living.

SPROUTED QUINOA TABBOULEH

PREPARATION TIME: 20 min

COOKING TIME: none

SERVINGS: 4

M.OF COOKING: No Cooking

INGREDIENTS:

- 1 C. sprouted quinoa
- 2 medium tomatoes, finely diced
- 1 cucumber, finely diced
- 4 green onions, sliced
- 1 C. fresh parsley, chopped
- 1/4 C. fresh mint, chopped
- Juice of 1 lemon
- 3 Tbls extra virgin olive oil
- Salt and pepper to taste

DIRECTIONS:

- Combine all ingredients in a large mixing bowl and toss to mix thoroughly
- Chill in the refrigerator for at least 15 minutes to allow flavors to meld
- Serve chilled or at room temperature

TIPS:

- Great served as a salad or a side dish
- For best flavor, let sit overnight in the refrigerator

N.V. : Calories: 222, Fat: 10g, Carbs: 28g, Protein: 6g, Sugar: 3g

HEIRLOOM BEAN CASSOULET

PREPARATION TIME: 15 min

COOKING TIME: 1 hr 30 min

SERVINGS: 6

M.OF COOKING: Baking

INGREDIENTS:

- 2 C. heirloom beans, soaked overnight
- 1 large onion, chopped
- 3 cloves garlic, minced
- 2 carrots, chopped
- 2 stalks celery, chopped
- 1 bay leaf
- 1 tsp smoked paprika
- 1/2 tsp dried thyme
- 4 C. vegetable stock
- 1 Tbls tomato paste
- Salt and pepper to taste

DIRECTIONS:

- Preheat oven to 350°F (175°C)
- In a Dutch oven, sauté onion, garlic, carrots, and celery until just softened
- Add soaked beans, bay leaf, smoked paprika, dried thyme, vegetable stock, and tomato paste and bring to a simmer
- Cover and transfer to oven
- Bake for 1 hr 30 min or until beans are tender
- Remove bay leaf before serving

TIPS:

- Serve with a crusty whole grain bread for a complete meal
- Can be made in advance and tastes even better the next day

N.V. : Calories: 315, Fat: 1.5g, Carbs: 58g, Protein: 19g, Sugar: 5g

BUCKWHEAT GROATS PILAF

PREPARATION TIME: 10 min

COOKING TIME: 20 min

SERVINGS: 4

M. OF COOKING: Stovetop

INGREDIENTS:

- 1 C. buckwheat groats
- 2 C. mushroom broth
- 1 medium onion, diced
- 1 Tbls coconut oil
- 1 tsp dried rosemary
- 1/2 tsp sea salt
- 1/4 tsp black pepper

DIRECTIONS:

- Over medium heat, sauté onion in coconut oil until translucent
- Add buckwheat groats and toast for 3-4 min, stirring constantly
- Add mushroom broth, dried rosemary, sea salt, and black pepper
- Bring to a boil, then reduce to a simmer and cover
- Cook for 20 min or until all liquid is absorbed and groats are fluffy

TIPS:

- Perfect as a side dish to accompany a range of proteins
- Add sautéed mushrooms for an extra savory flavor boost

N.V. : Calories: 160, Fat: 3g, Carbs: 30g, Protein: 6g, Sugar: 1g

AMARANTH PORRIDGE WITH SPICED PEAR

PREPARATION TIME: 5 min

COOKING TIME: 20 min

SERVINGS: 2

M. OF COOKING: Stovetop

INGREDIENTS:

- 1/2 C. amaranth
- 1 1/2 C. almond milk
- 1 ripe pear, cored and diced
- 1 tsp cinnamon
- 1/2 tsp nutmeg
- 1 Tbls maple syrup
- Pinch of salt

DIRECTIONS:

- In a saucepan, combine amaranth, almond milk, diced pear, cinnamon, nutmeg, and salt
- Bring to a boil, then reduce to a low simmer, stirring occasionally
- Cook for 20 min or until amaranth is creamy
- Stir in maple syrup before serving

TIPS:

- Garnish with a sprinkle of chopped nuts for added texture and protein
- Can use any seasonal fruit in place of pear

N.V. : Calories: 235, Fat: 4g, Carbs: 44g, Protein: 7g, Sugar: 12g

LENTIL MUJADARA

PREPARATION TIME: 10 min

COOKING TIME: 40 min

SERVINGS: 4

M. OF COOKING: Stovetop

INGREDIENTS:

- 1 C. brown lentils
- 1/2 C. bulgur wheat
- 2 large onions, thinly sliced
- 1/4 C. olive oil
- 2 tsp cumin seeds
- 4 C. water
- Salt and pepper to taste

DIRECTIONS:

- In a pot, bring water and lentils to a boil, then reduce to a simmer for 20 min
- In a separate pan, caramelize onions with olive oil over medium heat until golden brown

- Add cumin seeds to onions and sauté for 1 min

- Once lentils are partially cooked, add bulgur wheat and half of the caramelized onions and continue to cook for 20 min, or until all water is absorbed

- Season with salt and pepper and top with remaining onions to serve

TIPS:

- Pairs well with a dollop of Greek yogurt or cucumber raita

- To ensure even cooking, keep the heat on low when caramelizing the onions

N.V. : Calories: 320, Fat: 14g, Carbs: 40g, Protein: 12g, Sugar: 4g

BARLEY RISOTTO WITH ROASTED VEGETABLES

PREPARATION TIME: 15 min

COOKING TIME: 45 min

SERVINGS: 4

M. OF COOKING: Stovetop

INGREDIENTS:

- 1 C. pearled barley
- 4 C. vegetable stock
- 1 zucchini, diced
- 1 bell pepper, diced
- 1/2 red onion, diced
- 3 Tbls olive oil
- 1/2 C. grated Parmesan cheese
- 1 tsp dried basil
- Salt and black pepper to taste

DIRECTIONS:

- Preheat the oven to 400°F (200°C)

- Toss zucchini, bell pepper, and red onion with 1 Tbls olive oil and roast for 20 min

- In a saucepan, heat 2 Tbls olive oil and add barley, toasting for 3-4 min

- Gradually add vegetable stock, 1 C. at a time, stirring constantly and allowing barley to absorb liquid after each addition

- Once barley is tender and creamy, remove from heat, stir in roasted vegetables, Parmesan cheese, dried basil, salt, and black pepper

- Serve immediately

TIPS:

- Garnish with fresh herbs and an extra sprinkle of Parmesan for heightened flavor

- Leftovers can be stored in an airtight container and make excellent lunch options

N.V. : Calories: 350, Fat: 12g, Carbs: 51g, Protein: 10g, Sugar: 4g

SORGHUM SALAD WITH LEMON VINAIGRETTE

PREPARATION TIME: 10 min

COOKING TIME: 50 min

SERVINGS: 6

M. OF COOKING: Stovetop

INGREDIENTS:

- 2 C. sorghum grains
- 4 C. water
- 1 C. cherry tomatoes, halved
- 1/2 C. sliced cucumber
- 1/4 C. finely chopped red onion
- 1/4 C. chopped fresh basil
- 3 Tbls lemon juice
- 1 tsp lemon zest
- 1 garlic clove, minced
- 1/4 C. extra virgin olive oil
- Salt and pepper to taste

DIRECTIONS:

- Rinse sorghum grains and bring to a boil with water, then reduce to a simmer, cover, and cook for 50 min or until tender

- Drain excess water and cool to room temperature

- For the vinaigrette, whisk together lemon juice, lemon zest, minced garlic, olive oil, salt, and pepper
- Combine cooked sorghum, cherry tomatoes, cucumber, red onion, and fresh basil in a large bowl
- Drizzle with lemon vinaigrette and toss to coat evenly

- Chill for at least an hour before serving

TIPS:
- Can be served as a refreshing side or a light main dish
- Add crumbled feta or goat cheese for a creamy texture

N.V. : Calories: 290, Fat: 10g, Carbs: 47g, Protein: 7g, Sugar: 2g

9.3 CREATING YOUR OWN SPICE MIXES

The alchemy of cooking is never more enchanting than when mixing spices. In this twilight zone of flavors, a mere teaspoon can transport you through time and space, from the bustling bazaars of Morocco to the serene temples of India.

Crafting your own spice blends not only imbues your meals with vibrant flavor but also ensures you're leveraging the untapped healing properties of these ancient condiments. It's an empowering step towards self-sufficiency in your culinary adventures – a pinch of this, a dash of that, and you've got a secret weapon that transforms the simplest whole foods into divine creations.

In "Creating Your Own Spice Mixes," we'll peel back the curtain to reveal the simplicity behind the complex taste profiles that elevate our dishes. Together, we'll discover that with a foundation of a few core spices, your kitchen can house an endless tapestry of flavor, ready to bring warmth, depth, and nutrition to every meal.

SUNNY HERB DE PROVENCE

PREPARATION TIME: 5 min
COOKING TIME: none
SERVINGS: About 4 oz
M.OF COOKING: No Cooking
INGREDIENTS:
- 2 Tbls dried savory
- 2 Tbls dried rosemary
- 2 Tbls dried thyme
- 2 Tbls dried oregano
- 2 Tbls dried basil
- 1 Tbls dried marjoram
- 1 Tbls fennel seeds
- 1 tsp dried lavender flowers
- 1 tsp dried tarragon

DIRECTIONS:
- Crush fennel seeds lightly to release flavor
- Combine all herbs and store in an airtight container away from direct sunlight

TIPS:
- Use as a rub for grilling or roasting meats and vegetables
- Can be steeped in olive oil for a fragrant dip or dressing

N.V. : Calories: 8 per tsp, Fat: 0.2g, Carbs: 1.5g, Protein: 0.3g, Sugar: 0g

ZESTY JAMAICAN JERK SEASONING

PREPARATION TIME: 10 min

COOKING TIME: none

SERVINGS: About 5 oz

M.OF COOKING: No Cooking

INGREDIENTS:

- 1 Tbls onion powder
- 2 Tbls garlic powder
- 2 tsp cayenne pepper
- 1 Tbls ground allspice
- 2 tsp smoked paprika
- 1 tsp ground nutmeg
- 1 tsp cinnamon
- 2 Tbls dried thyme
- 1 Tbls sugar
- 1 tsp dried crushed red pepper
- 2 tsp sea salt
- 1 tsp ground black pepper

DIRECTIONS:

- Combine all ingredients until homogenous
- Store in a dry, airtight container away from heat and light

TIPS:

- Can be used on any protein, mix with lime juice for a marinade
- Adjust cayenne pepper if a milder heat level is desired

N.V. : Calories: 10 per tsp, Fat: 0.2g, Carbs: 2g, Protein: 0.3g, Sugar: 0.5g

BOLD ETHIOPIAN BERBERE

PREPARATION TIME: 15 min

COOKING TIME: none

SERVINGS: About 4 oz

M.OF COOKING: No Cooking

INGREDIENTS:

- 2 Tbls chili powder
- 2 Tbls paprika
- 1 Tbls salt
- 1 tsp ground fenugreek
- 1 tsp ground ginger
- 1 tsp onion powder
- ½ tsp ground cardamom
- ½ tsp ground coriander
- ¼ tsp ground nutmeg
- ¼ tsp garlic powder
- ¼ tsp ground cloves
- ¼ tsp ground cinnamon
- ¼ tsp ground allspice

DIRECTIONS:

- Mix all spices thoroughly until well combined
- Store in an airtight jar in a cool, dark place

TIPS:

- Excellent for stews and grilling, use sparingly as it is very potent
- A cornerstone in traditional Ethiopian dishes such as Doro Wat

N.V. : Calories: 16 per Tbls, Fat: 0.7g, Carbs: 3g, Protein: 0.8g, Sugar: 0.2g

MELLOW GARAM MASALA

PREPARATION TIME: 10 min

COOKING TIME: none

SERVINGS: About 3 oz

M.OF COOKING: No Cooking

INGREDIENTS:

- 2 Tbls ground cumin
- 2 Tbls ground coriander
- 2 Tbls ground cardamom
- 1 Tbls ground black pepper
- 1 Tbls ground cinnamon
- 1 tsp ground cloves
- 1 tsp ground nutmeg

DIRECTIONS:

- Blend all spices until completely mixed
- Store in a cool, dark place in a tightly sealed container

TIPS:

- Use as a finishing spice to retain flavor, particularly in curries and soups
- Gently toast spices before grinding for a more robust flavor

N.V. : Calories: 18 per Tbls, Fat: 0.9g, Carbs: 3.3g, Protein: 0.6g, Sugar: 0.1g

SMOKY BBQ DRY RUB

PREPARATION TIME: 5 min
COOKING TIME: none
SERVINGS: About 6 oz
M.OF COOKING: No Cooking
INGREDIENTS:
- ¼ C. smoked paprika
- ¼ C. brown sugar
- 1 Tbls salt
- 1 Tbls chili powder
- 1 Tbls garlic powder
- 1 Tbls onion powder
- 1 Tbls ground mustard
- 1 tsp cumin
- 1 tsp ground black pepper
- ½ tsp cayenne pepper

DIRECTIONS:
- Mix all ingredients together until there are no clumps
- Store in an airtight jar to maintain smoky flavor

TIPS:
- Ideal rub for pork, brisket, and ribs before smoking or grilling
- Adjust the amount of cayenne to control the heat level

N.V. : Calories: 12 per tsp, Fat: 0.2g, Carbs: 2.8g, Protein: 0.3g, Sugar: 2g

ITALIAN AMMOGLIO SAUCE MIX

PREPARATION TIME: 5 min
COOKING TIME: none
SERVINGS: About 3 oz
M.OF COOKING: No Cooking

INGREDIENTS:
- 2 Tbls dried oregano
- 2 Tbls dried basil
- 2 Tbls dried parsley
- 1 Tbls dried rosemary
- 2 tsp garlic powder
- 2 tsp salt
- 1 tsp ground black pepper
- 1 tsp dried crushed red pepper
- 1 tsp dried sage

DIRECTIONS:
- Combine all dried herbs and spices until evenly mixed
- Store in an airtight container to preserve the aromatic flavors

TIPS:
- Mix with olive oil and vinegar for a fresh Italian sauce, perfect for dipping bread
- Can also be sprinkled on pizza and pasta dishes

N.V. : Calories: 5 per tsp, Fat: 0.1g, Carbs: 1.2g, Protein: 0.2g, Sugar: 0g

FRENCH BOUQUET GARNI BLEND

PREPARATION TIME: 5 min
COOKING TIME: none
SERVINGS: Makes 10 bundles
M.OF COOKING: No Cooking
INGREDIENTS:
- 20 bay leaves
- 20 sprigs of fresh thyme
- 10 sprigs of fresh parsley
- 10 pieces of leek leaves or cheesecloth

DIRECTIONS:
- Place one bay leaf, two sprigs of thyme, and one sprig of parsley onto leek leaf and tie securely with kitchen twine
- Store in a dry place until needed

TIPS:

- Primarily used in soups, stews and stock, remove bundle before serving
- Fresh herbs will dry naturally tied in bundle, enhancing the fusion of flavors

N.V. : Varies based on application, Varies based on application, Varies based on application, Varies based on application, Varies based on application, Varies based on application

10.1 STRATEGIES FOR EFFICIENT MEAL PREP

In the rhythm of our fast-paced lives, the art of meal prepping emerges as a beacon of organization and peace. It is the bridge that connects our nourishing ambitions with the practicality of everyday living. You might think of meal prepping as a weekly ceremony, a little time set aside to pay homage to the body's needs and the family's contentment. Dive into this chapter with the intention to merge the benefits of whole foods with your dynamic lifestyle by embracing strategies that simplify meal preparation.

Consider meal prepping an investment, one that pays you back in health dividends, rich flavors, and precious time saved. The motto here is clear: prepare once, eat nutritiously numerous times. Let's equip you with a blueprint for turning your kitchen endeavors into a streamlined process, teeming with wholesome goodness.

Understand Your Canvas

Each week is your canvas; you decide what your meal masterpiece looks like. Start by knowing how many meals you need, accounting for breakfasts, lunches, dinners, and snacks. Keep in mind the number of servings – family size matters here. This doesn't mean crafting complex spreadsheets; it can be as simple as jotting down a rough count on a notepad.

Choose Versatility

Embrace foods that wear many hats. Quinoa, for example, can be your breakfast porridge, your lunch salad base, or a dinner side. Vegetables like bell peppers and zucchini can find their way into stir-fry dishes, salads, and casseroles. By choosing versatile ingredients, you reduce prep time, cost, and kitchen chaos.

Shop Smart

Armed with your versatile staples list, shop with precision. Local farmers' markets are whole food havens, but don't be discouraged if you're bound to the supermarket. Look for the fresh, the seasonal, and the least processed. Buy nuts and seeds in bulk—but be wary of perishables. If it grows from the earth and boasts a rich color, it's likely a friend of whole foods.

Plan for Protein

Plant-based or not, your protein is the cornerstone of satiety in your meals. Prepare a variety of beans, lentils, tofu, or if you're an omnivore, a selection of lean meats or fish, ahead of time. These can be effortlessly added to any meal to enhance its nutritional profile.

Batch Cook with a Twist

Consider cooking large quantities not as a chore, but as a clever hack to preserve time and energy. Make large pots of soup, stews, or grains, but don't stop there. Add different spices, herbs, or vegetables to smaller batches, so the same brown rice can feel new in each dish with a sprinkle of cilantro here or a pinch of curry there.

Keep It Fresh

Salads needn't be soggy affairs of wilted greens. Keep ingredients separate and assemble them fresh. Make use of mason jars for layering; the dressing at the bottom, followed by sturdier veggies or grains, finally topped with leafy greens. The simple shake before eating brings your salad to life.

Harness the Power of Freezing

Freezing is the unsung hero of meal prep. Cooked grains, soups, patties, or balls—most fare well in the cold. While nutrition can suffer in storage, freezing retains most of the goodness. Label everything—you're not seeking mystery meals in your future.

Delight in Dressings and Dips

Those little jars of homemade dressings and dips? They're goldmines. The simplicity of a basic olive oil, vinegar, mustard, and herb dressing can elevate a dish from bland to grand. Hummus or guacamole can bring life to vegetables or whole grain crackers. Preparing these ahead means instant flavor upgrades.

Embrace Leftovers

There's nobility in using leftovers; they're the stalwarts of quick lunches or hassle-free dinners. Yesterday's roasted vegetables are today's pureed soup. Some would argue they taste better the second time around, as their flavors have melded and matured.

Customize Your Containers

Not all containers are created equal. Glass or BPA-free containers with compartments can inspire serving size discipline and keep foods from unwanted mingling. With clear containers, your fridge becomes a gallery of ready-to-eat meals, colorful and inviting.

Utilize Tools and Appliances

Let modern marvels assist you—the food processor, the slow cooker, the instant pot, the blender. Each has a role to play in expediting meal prep. Chopping can be minutes work, beans can stew to perfection without a watchful eye, and smoothies are but a button push away.

Stagger Your Prep

Meal prepping needn't consume your Sunday. Stagger your prep during the week if the load feels too heavy. Roast your nuts and seeds Tuesday, wash and chop your veggies on Thursday. This way, the kitchen doesn't feel like an assembly line, but a space of constant, manageable activity.

Incorporate Leftover Prep into Meal Time

Why not chop extra onions while preparing tonight's dinner? Why not double your quinoa, knowing full-well a wrap beckons tomorrow? This kind of forward-thinking during regular meal times shrinks your dedicated prep time and opens margins in your daily schedule.

Stay Flexible

Your meal plan is a guide, not a dictator. Unexpected events happen, taste buds yearn for change. If Thursday calls for soup but the heart cries for a salad, by all means, make the swap. The joy of meal prep lies not just in its structure but in its malleable nature, conforming to life's ebb and flow.

Make It a Family Affair

Invite your family into this world of meal preparation. Assign tasks, teach techniques, and share the importance of whole foods. Children who dip their hands into the warmth of meal prep grow to appreciate their meals deeply. They become guardians of their own health.

This ritual of meal prep is your gateway to honoring the whole food philosophy in the everyday. Think of these strategies not as rules but as companions on your whole food voyage. They're there to carry some of the load so that the journey is less arduous and infinitely more enjoyable.

In mastery of these strategies, you'll find the forge of your own creativity. Whole foods will no longer be intimidating; they'll be the familiar pathways of succulence in your kitchen. You'll learn the dance—the chopping, the blending, the seasoning—with grace and precision. And you'll pass on these moves to your family, to your friends, and who knows, perhaps to generations who also dream of a life in harmonious coexistence with nature's provisions.

Turn the page expecting to nourish not just your body but your soul. For as you begin to weave these strategies into your weekly rhythms, you'll uncover the true power that meal prepping has— in bestowing upon you the gift of time, health, and, most of all, peace of mind.

10.2 STORING AND PRESERVING FRESHNESS

Embracing the art of meal prepping is like casting a spell of simplicity over your weekly dining ritual—it's about making the act of eating nutrient-dense, whole foods a seamless part of your dynamic life. As enchanting as meal prepping can be, its true sorcery lies in the gentle art of storing and preserving the freshness of your ingredients. After all, what's the point of dedicating a Sunday afternoon to prepping if your vibrant veggies turn lackluster by Tuesday?

The linchpin to maintaining the spirit of your carefully planned meals lies in understanding how to keep your produce, proteins, and prepared meals tasting as though they were made moments ago—even days after their creation. Let's embark on a journey through the foundational techniques of food storage that will ensure your meal prepping efforts stand the test of time.

Firstly, consider the containers you choose as the guardians of freshness. Glass containers are the shining knights in this arena—transparent, non-porous, and steadfast, they don't absorb flavors or smells. Plus, their ability to go from fridge to oven to dishwasher makes them champions of convenience. BPA-free plastic containers can also serve well, particularly those designed with seal-tight lids. And let's not forget silicone storage bags—reusable, versatile, and perfect for those who like to squeeze every bit of air out to thwart the devious advances of food spoilage.

But it's not just about picking the right container; it's about understanding the unique needs of each food group. Let's delve into the specifics:

Fruits and Vegetables

Fresh produce breathes, almost as if alive, and this necessitates an understanding of their respiration. Ethylene-producing fruits like apples, bananas, and tomatoes can hasten the ripening (and over-ripening) of neighboring fruits and veggies. Store these catalysts of ripeness separately, and embrace the crisper drawer—it's tailored to maintain an Eden for your greens.

Greens, with their featherlight leaves, crave moisture. Enclose them in containers lined with a paper towel to absorb excess humidity. Root vegetables, on the other hand, prefer a dark, cool space away from the light of day, while herbs like basil are sun seekers and will bask on your counter if given a water bath to dip their stems.

Proteins

Here, the rule of 'first in, first out,' applies with an iron will. Cooked proteins should only be invited to stay in your fridge for a span of three to four days. After this time, their vitality wanes. The freezer, though, can be a haven for proteins, but only if you take care to wrap them properly—airtight and with the cautious use of freezer bags.

Grains and Legumes

Whole grains and legumes, those hearty souls, are best kept in airtight containers and in the cooler temperatures and shadows of your pantry. They are a patient lot; however, be sure to check on them periodically, as they can fall afoul of moisture or pests if neglected.

Prepared Meals

With prepared meals, consider portioning as your strategy for triumph. Storing single servings not only makes for easy grab-and-go options but also reduces the number of times you expose the entire batch of food to the air—each opening an invitation to decay.

A word on cooling: Allow your cooked masterpieces to cool to room temperature before giving them sanctuary in the fridge. This wards off condensation, which left unchecked, would summon unwanted bacteria with its siren call of moisture.

The Freezer's Role

The freezer is an ally of great resource but wield it wisely. Freeze food flat and evenly when possible to quicken the thawing process later, and label everything with dates and contents. Clarity is kindness in the realm of meal prepping.

Timing and Temperature

Timing is as crucial as temperature. Refrigerators should reside at or below 40°F, the threshold where bacterial growth slows to a languid pace. The freezer's magic number is 0°F, the realm of suspended animation for food.

The Dance of Rotation

There's a grace to the rotation of inventory, ensuring older items dance their way to the front, ready to be consumed first. It's this dance that maintains the vibrancy and variety of your meals.

Refresh and Revitalize

Once thawed or brought back to the world of warmth, meals may need a touch of magic to revitalize. A splash of liquid, a sprinkle of herbs, or the briefest kiss of heat can reawaken flavors and textures, ensuring each repast is as pleasurable as its first presentation.

The Power of Preservation

And lastly, there's the enchantment of other preservation methods—the brine of pickling, the culture of fermenting, and the reduction of sauces. These aren't only about extending the life of your whole foods; they are methods of transformation, elevating the ordinary to extraordinary.

In this elegant waltz of whole food meal prepping, you become the orchestrator of time and taste. It's a role that's both practical and profound as you take control of your nourishment, ensuring that every bite you and your loved ones take is as fresh and life-affirming as nature intended.

By following these guidelines, you protect not merely the substance of your food but its soul. When you unveil a dish from its container days after its making, it should still sing with the vibrant hues, crisp textures, and lush flavors that nature gifted it with. This practice of storing and preserving the freshness of your meals is both an act of love and a declaration of independence from the tyranny of takeout and processed foods.

Make no mistake, meal prepping is an investment—an investment in time, in health, in family. But like all good investments, it rewards you manifold. With these methods, you won't merely save time and eat healthier; you'll also pay homage to the ingredients, honoring their journey from earth to table. And, with each mouthful, you'll taste the crispness of care, the seasoning of foresight, and the deep, abiding flavor of well-being.

10.3 SAMPLE WEEKLY MEAL PLANS

Embarking on a whole food journey can be a transformative experience not just for you, but for your loved ones as well. It's about learning to harness the power of nature's wellness in the coziness of your own kitchen, creating a healthful haven for everyone who gathers around your table. Your commitment to a whole food lifestyle doesn't have to collide with the fast-paced beat of modern life. Instead, let's explore how proper planning can align your nutrition goals with your schedule, making the seemingly impossible utterly attainable.

Imagine this: it's a bustling Wednesday evening, and instead of resorting to takeout or processed convenience foods, you're unwrapping a homemade whole-grain quiche that you prepared over the weekend. This isn't just a daydream, it's the reality that awaits with a well-thought-out meal plan.

First things first, let's demystify the elusive aura surrounding meal plans. Far from being rigid dietary dictators, think of meal plans as your customizable roadmap to culinary success. They take into account your time limitations, budget constraints, and the intricate tastes of your family. The happy byproduct? Less food waste, reduced stress during grocery shopping, and the joy of never having to answer "What's for dinner?" at the end of a long day.

The Art of Meal Planning

A meal plan is more than just a list of dishes. It's a strategic puzzle where every meal fits into your week with purpose and intent. By accounting for breakfast, lunch, dinner, and snacks, we're setting the stage for nutritional harmony.

Imagine a table laden with colors, textures, and nutrients, with each meal complementing the next. Now let's bring that vision to life, one week at a time.

Crafting Your Weekly Whole Food Symphony

Monday: Begin your week with intention. A vibrant green smoothie sets the tone for a day charged with vitality. For lunch, let's introduce a salad kissed by the sun – think leafy greens, sprouted beans, and a handful of nuts, all dressed in a tangy citrus vinaigrette. As the evening rolls around, gather your family for a soul-satisfying vegetable stir-fry over quinoa, infusing both warmth and wellness into your night.

Tuesday: As dawn breaks, nourish your body with a bowl of steel-cut oats, adorned with slices of seasonal fruit and a sprinkle of chia seeds. Midday approaches, and with it, a hearty bowl of lentil soup that you've cleverly batch-cooked the day prior. Dinner is a dance of flavors, with baked sweet potatoes and a side of steamed broccoli, a meal humble in its ingredients but rich in nutrition.

Wednesday: The midweek hustle could use an energy boost. Blend a banana with a generous pour of homemade nut milk and a spoonful of almond butter for a breakfast smoothie that fuels your stride. Lunch features those delightful wraps you prepped ahead, their whole grain encasing vibrant veggies and hummus. As twilight descends, a roasted chicken (if you incline toward meat) alongside a medley of roasted root vegetables fills your home with an aroma that beckons all to the table.

Thursday: Breakfast is a nod to simplicity: a parfait of yogurt, homemade granola, and a cascade of berries. Come lunch, reimagine last night's chicken as a salad dressing, tossed with fresh greens and avocado slices. Dinner unfolds with Mother Nature's bounty, presenting a plant-based platter starring grilled eggplant, zucchini, and bell peppers.

Friday: Well into your rhythm, breakfast is swift with a slice of whole grain toast, ripe avocado, and a poached egg. A quinoa salad, vibrant and abundant with vegetables, awaits at lunch, its flavors having melded beautifully overnight. Closing your workweek is a celebration – a fish grilled to perfection (for those who prefer their protein from the sea), cradled by a side of farro salad punctuated with herbs.

Saturday: The weekend air is relaxed and so is your breakfast. A modest spread of nut butter on sprouted grain bread with a side of apple slices wakes up your palate. Lunch is a playful affair with those nutritious dips and spreads you prepared, surrounded by an army of fresh veggie sticks. Dinner embraces the joy of sharing with make-your-own-burrito bowls, an assembly of brown rice, beans, salsa, and guacamole waiting for each family member's creative touch.

Sunday: The day of rest begins with a smoothie bowl, its surface a canvas for your favorite seeds and nuts. Lunch is light yet fulfilling, a clear broth soup perhaps with whispers of ginger, garlic, and a tangle of vegetable noodles. Your week concludes with an ode to tradition – a slow-cooked stew, a harmony of root vegetables, legumes, and aromatic herbs.

Flexibility and Fluidity - The Keys to Sustainable Meal Planning

Life is unpredictable, and sometimes plans pivot. That's why our sample meal plan is not a script but a guide, leaving room for flexibility. Swap out a lunch for last night's leftovers or shuffle the days as you please. The underlying goal is to have a framework that celebrates whole foods, respects your time, and nourishes your family's health.

Beyond the Meals - Embracing Seasons and Sales

A smart meal planner is a savvy shopper. Attuning your meal plans to seasonal produce does wonders for both your palate and purse. Farmers' markets can be treasure troves for fresh, affordable whole foods, and keeping an eye on supermarket sales helps stock up your pantry with staples that have a longer shelf life, such as whole grains and legumes.

Prep, Prep, Prep!

Yes, the secret sauce to seamless meal plans is, undeniably, preparation. Allotting a chunk of your weekend or any off day to pre-cooking grains, chopping vegetables, or preparing protein helps turn your meal plan into an easy-to-follow, paint-by-numbers kitchen escapade throughout the week.

Meal Planning as a Family Affair

Involving your household in meal planning fosters a sense of ownership and excitement around meal times. Have your family members voice their favorite whole food dishes, and include their selections in your weekly plan. This inclusivity turns the act of eating into a communal joy and can encourage healthier eating habits for all.

Let this weekly meal plan serve merely as a foundation, a springboard from which you'll embark on a culinary journey filled with whole food delights. Your voyage will be unique, dotted with the preferences, schedules, and tastes that define your life. With a little foresight and creativity, you'll find yourself sailing through weeks where whole foods aren't just an aspiration, but a delicious reality. And as you journey forth, let the principles of variety, nutrition, and simplicity illuminate your path to eating well, living well, and in turn, flourishing.

CHAPTER 11: 30-DAY WHOLE FOOD MEAL PLAN

11.1 WEEK 1: INTRODUCTION AND EASY START

Embarking on a whole food journey marks the beginning of a transformative path towards health and well-being. Week 1: Introduction and Easy Start is designed to ease you into the world of whole foods, focusing on simplicity, nutrition, and flavor. This week, we emphasize meals that are both nourishing and straightforward to prepare, introducing your palate to the rich tastes and textures of unprocessed ingredients. From energizing breakfasts to satisfying dinners, each recipe is chosen to provide balanced nutrients while celebrating the natural goodness of whole foods. Snacks are crafted to keep energy levels steady throughout the day. As we lay the foundation for a healthier lifestyle, this week's plan encourages mindful eating, culinary exploration, and a deeper connection with your food.

WEEK 1	breakfast	snack	lunch	snack	dinner
Monday	Golden Turmeric Morning Elixir	Crispy Kale Chips with Tahini Drizzle	Crispy Rainbow Kale Salad with Miso Tahini Dressing	Spicy Roasted Chickpeas	Socca Pizza with Sun-Dried Tomato Pesto
Tuesday	Avocado Matcha Chiller	Rainbow Carrot and Zucchini Ribbons with Chia Seeds	Avocado & Grapefruit Quinoa Salad with Adobo Lime Dressing	Zucchini and Carrot Fritters	Grilled Portobello Steaks with Avocado Chimichurri
Wednesday	Spiced Pear Breakfast Quinoa Bowl	Avocado and Tomato Stuffed Cucumber Boats	Spelt Berry Salad with Roasted Poblano Vinaigrette	Crispy Kale Chips with Nutritional Yeast	Roasted Rainbow Bowl with Tahini Drizzle
Thursday	Beetroot and Berry Energizer	Multigrain Rosemary and Sea Salt Crackers	Shaved Brussels Sprout Caesar with Cashew-Parm Crisps	Roasted Carrot Hummus	Spiced Lentil Stuffed Acorn Squash
Friday	Spirulina Sunrise Smoothie	Sesame Spelt Crackers	Warm Lentil Salad with Charred Leeks Vinaigrette	Beet and Walnut Pâté	Cauliflower Steaks with Romesco Sauce
Saturday	Cherry Almond Sunrise Bowl	Quinoa Chia Seed Crackers	Curried Chickpea Salad Wrap	Spicy Avocado and Chia Guacamole	Zucchini Noodle Pad Thai
Sunday	Tri-Grain Apple Cinnamon Porridge	Pumpkin Seed Amaranth Crackers	Rustic White Bean and Fennel Soup	Miso Aubergine Spread	Citrus-Herb Grilled Trout

Week 2: Diverse Flavors and Ingredients invites you on a global culinary journey, right from your kitchen. This week is designed to broaden your palate, incorporating a mosaic of flavors and ingredients that celebrate the diversity of whole foods. From the aromatic spices of India to the bold textures of Mediterranean cuisine, each meal is a new adventure. As we delve deeper into the world of whole foods, we embrace the opportunity to explore unfamiliar ingredients, experiment with different cooking methods, and discover new favorites. This week, let's cherish the joy of cooking and eating as an exploration, an opportunity to nourish our bodies with a spectrum of vibrant, healthful, and delicious meals.

WEEK 2	breakfast	snack	lunch	snack	dinner
Monday	Amaranth Porridge with Spiced Pear	Crispy Kale Chips with Tahini Drizzle	Heirloom Bean Cassoulet	Sesame Spelt Crackers	Barley Risotto with Roasted Vegetables
Tuesday	Buckwheat Groats Pilaf	Rainbow Carrot and Zucchini Ribbons with Chia Seeds	Lentil Mujadara	Zucchini and Carrot Fritters	Socca Pizza with Sun-Dried Tomato Pesto
Wednesday	Golden Turmeric Morning Elixir	Multigrain Rosemary and Sea Salt Crackers	Crispy Rainbow Kale Salad with Miso Tahini Dressing	Roasted Carrot Hummus	Roasted Rainbow Bowl with Tahini Drizzle
Thursday	Avocado Matcha Chiller	Pumpkin Seed Amaranth Crackers	Shaved Brussels Sprout Caesar with Cashew-Parm Crisps	Beet and Walnut Pâté	Spiced Lentil Stuffed Acorn Squash
Friday	Spiced Pear Breakfast Quinoa Bowl	Quinoa Chia Seed Crackers	Warm Lentil Salad with Charred Leeks Vinaigrette	Spicy Avocado and Chia Guacamole	Cauliflower Steaks with Romesco Sauce
Saturday	Beetroot and Berry Energizer	Avocado and Tomato Stuffed Cucumber Boats	Avocado & Grapefruit Quinoa Salad with Adobo Lime Dressing	Spicy Roasted Chickpeas	Zucchini Noodle Pad Thai
Sunday	Spirulina Sunrise Smoothie	Miso Aubergine Spread	Curried Chickpea Salad Wrap	Crispy Kale Chips with Nutritional Yeast	Citrus-Herb Grilled Trout

11.3 WEEK 3: EXPERIMENTING WITH RECIPES

Week 3: Experimenting with Recipes is an invitation to step out of your culinary comfort zone and embrace the art of experimentation. This week is about discovering the joy of mixing and matching ingredients, exploring new cooking methods, and perhaps even creating a few dishes of your own. Each day's menu is designed to inspire creativity and curiosity in the kitchen, utilizing whole foods in innovative ways that surprise and delight the palate. From savory breakfasts to indulgent dinners, the focus is on enjoying the process of cooking as much as the results. Let's embark on this adventure with an open mind and an eager stomach, ready to taste the unexpected and revel in the homemade.

WEEK 3	breakfast	snack	lunch	snack	dinner
Monday	Buckwheat Blueberry Lemon Pancakes	Crispy Kale Chips with Nutritional Yeast	Crispy Rainbow Kale Salad with Miso Tahini Dressing	Sesame Spelt Crackers	Spelt Berry Salad with Roasted Poblano Vinaigrette
Tuesday	Spiced Teff Porridge with Dried Fruit Compote	Rainbow Carrot and Zucchini Ribbons with Chia Seeds	Shaved Brussels Sprout Caesar with Cashew-Parm Crisps	Avocado and Tomato Stuffed Cucumber Boats	Warm Lentil Salad with Charred Leeks Vinaigrette
Wednesday	Tri-Grain Apple Cinnamon Porridge	Multigrain Rosemary and Sea Salt Crackers	Avocado & Grapefruit Quinoa Salad with Adobo Lime Dressing	Roasted Carrot Hummus	Quinoa Tabbouleh with Charred Corn
Thursday	Millet and Chia Seed Pancakes	Pumpkin Seed Amaranth Crackers	Kaleidoscope Quinoa Salad	Beet and Walnut Pâté	Millet Pilaf with Roasted Root Vegetables
Friday	Amaranth Pumpkin Porridge	Quinoa Chia Seed Crackers	Moroccan Lentil and Chickpea Stew	Spicy Avocado and Chia Guacamole	Buckwheat with Caramelized Shallots and Swiss Chard
Saturday	Wild Rice Apple Pancakes with Cinnamon	Avocado and Tomato Stuffed Cucumber Boats	Thai Coconut Curry Butternut Squash Soup	Spicy Roasted Chickpeas	Farro with Grilled Asparagus and Lemon Zest
Sunday	Golden Turmeric Morning Elixir	Miso Aubergine Spread	Rustic White Bean and Fennel Soup	Crispy Kale Chips with Tahini Drizzle	Toasted Quinoa with Roasted Butternut Squash

11.4 WEEK 4: ADVANCED PREPARATIONS AND COMBINATIONS

"Advanced Preparations and Combinations" marks the culmination of our culinary journey, challenging us to apply all we've learned in a celebration of flavors, techniques, and whole foods. This week, we delve into intricate recipes that demand a bit more time and effort but promise rewarding tastes and health benefits. The focus is on batch cooking, creative seasoning, and the art of food pairing, designed to streamline your cooking process while diversifying your palate. As we explore the harmony between different foods and learn to prepare meals that can be easily combined or transformed throughout the week, we embrace the joy of cooking as an essential part of a wholesome lifestyle. Let's embark on this final week with enthusiasm, ready to experiment and enjoy the delicious, nutritious meals we create.

WEEK 4	breakfast	snack	lunch	snack	dinner
Monday	Chia & Berry Gelato	Herbed Oat and Teff Crackers	Kaleidoscope Quinoa Salad	Roasted Carrot Hummus	Socca Pizza with Sun-Dried Tomato Pesto
Tuesday	Grilled Peach with Cinnamon Honey Drizzle	Multigrain Rosemary and Sea Salt Crackers	Shaved Brussels Sprout Caesar with Cashew-Parm Crisps	Beet and Walnut Pâté	Grilled Portobello Steaks with Avocado Chimichurri
Wednesday	Frozen Berry Yogurt Bark	Sesame Spelt Crackers	Warm Lentil Salad with Charred Leeks Vinaigrette	Spicy Avocado and Chia Guacamole	Roasted Rainbow Bowl with Tahini Drizzle
Thursday	Fig and Walnut Stuffed Apples	Pumpkin Seed Amaranth Crackers	Crispy Rainbow Kale Salad with Miso Tahini Dressing	Sun-Dried Tomato and Cannellini Bean Dip	Spiced Lentil Stuffed Acorn Squash
Friday	Papaya Lime Sorbet	Quinoa Chia Seed Crackers	Avocado & Grapefruit Quinoa Salad with Adobo Lime Dressing	Lemony Artichoke and Herb Dip	Cauliflower Steaks with Romesco Sauce
Saturday	Avocado Chocolate Mousse with Raspberries	Avocado and Tomato Stuffed Cucumber Boats	Curried Chickpea Salad Wrap	Spicy Roasted Chickpeas	Zucchini Noodle Pad Thai
Sunday	Pear Ginger Compote with Crunchy Quinoa	Miso Aubergine Spread	Rustic White Bean and Fennel Soup	Crispy Kale Chips with Nutritional Yeast	Citrus-Herb Grilled Trout

Made in the USA
Las Vegas, NV
01 June 2024